SURF FISHING
THE ATLANTIC COAST

SURF FISHING
THE ATLANTIC COAST

Eric B. Burnley

Foreword by George Reiger

Stackpole Books

Copyright © 1989 by Stackpole Books

Published by
STACKPOLE BOOKS
Cameron and Kelker Streets
P.O. Box 1831
Harrisburg, PA 17105

Printed in the United States of America

10 9 8 7 6 5 4 3 2 1

First Edition

Library of Congress Cataloging-in-Publication Data

Burnley, Eric B.
    Surf fishing the Atlantic coast / Eric B. Burnley: foreword by
George Reiger.
        p.   c.m.
    Includes index.
    ISBN 0-8117-2301-1
    1. Surf fishing—Atlantic Coast (U.S.)   I. Title.
SH464.A85B87   1989
799.1'6614—dc19

88-39541
CIP

Jacket design by Tracy Patterson
Book design by Art Unlimited
Illustrated by Bob Jones

To my wife Barbara, who is much more than my better half; and to my brother Jay, who would have shared so much of this had he been given the time.

CONTENTS

FOREWORD

One golden age in surf fishing is gone. That involved unlimited shore access and countless miles of open beach explored with old Model A trucks rigged for fishing and camping.

A new golden age is dawning. It involves piers and bridges specifically designed for fishermen, superior tackle, and sound advice from a dedicated band of knowledgeable outdoor writers.

There is magic in the surf that draws back even dedicated bluewater anglers. After all, offshore fishing is a team sport with little sense of individual achievement, except for the skipper. Surf fishing, on the other hand, is very much a matter of solitary success. It's the saltwater equivalent of deer hunting. And just as the best deer hunters get their trophy bucks season after season, the best surf fishermen get their trophy channel bass and stripers year after year—and then release them to make sure they'll be there the following year.

Eric Burnley personifies the new golden age. He is familiar with the latest tackle and techniques, yet equally well versed in older time-tested methods. He is an articulate spokesman for shore fishermen's rights and a better angling environment. He is energetic, imaginative, and the late great surf fisherman, Al Reinfelder, would have called him "true hungry." This book is a fine—nay, necessary—addition to any serious surf fisherman's library.

George Reiger, author of
Profiles in Saltwater Angling
and *Wanderer on My Native Shore*

CHAPTER 1

WHY WE FISH
THE SURF

All fishermen must be optimistic about their chances of success but none so much as the surf fisherman. His quarry is unrestricted in movement while he must stand his ground on the beach. While freshwater bass or trout anglers know the fish are going to be available whenever they choose to go after them, the surf fisherman may wait months for his fish to show up, only to have a strong storm keep them away from the beach and out of his territory.

The advances in fishing technology that have aided the boat fisherman have done little to help the surf caster. He cannot rely on fish finders, radar, or loran to locate productive fishing spots. He must use his own skills and experience to interpret the weather outlook, surf conditions, tide and current direction, and other factors in order to pick a place where he thinks the fish may show up. Unfortunately, the fish do not always interpret these conditions the same way the surf fisherman does and they may decide to show up somewhere else or not at all.

Surf fishermen, by necessity, must become more involved in their sport than do most other anglers. The dry-fly trout angler studies not only the fish but is also a devout student of the insect life on his favorite stream. He must know when hatches will occur and be able to tie flies that imitate the emerging insects. The accomplished surf fisherman will know not only when the big channel bass or stripers will move along the coast, but what they will be feeding on and how to catch or imitate this bait. A big gamester in the surf can be as particular about his feeding habits as any native brown trout.

The inherent difficulty of catching a fish in the surf is the challenge accepted by the surf fisherman. Most of us could fish in other places using other methods, and although our success would not be assured, it would be a much safer bet than are the odds on surf fishing. The payoff comes in the excitement and exhilaration of beating the odds and beaching a trophy fish.

Challenge is the motivating force behind many surf fishermen but it is far from the only reason we venture forth. The wild beauty of the sea, something humans still cannot control, draws us to the beach. We can stand face to face with an ocean that has the ability to destroy us and all that we have built along its shore. We can look upon waters that touch continents from the Arctic to the Antarctic. We can contemplate the thoughts of other surf fishermen who have entirely different backgrounds but who are also drawn to the edge of the ocean. There is for me and, I suspect, for most other surf fishermen a feeling of contentment when we stand in the wash, rod in hand, mind clear of the troubling thoughts of daily life.

Fishing in the surf does not solve any problems but it does provide a release, a safe harbor where troubles are kept behind the reef, on the outside of the bar, and we can rest and regain our strength before venturing again on the sea of life.

David Deuel with his 94-pound 2-ounce World Record red drum, taken from the beach of Avon, North Carolina

Dare County Tourist Bureau photo.

CHAPTER 2

TACKLE

The correct tackle may not guarantee success but it will make you more comfortable while you wait for the fish. It will also give you a reasonable expectation of catching one when they finally make an appearance.

There are certain physical characteristics of surf that require specific types of tackle. You must be able to cast your bait or lure beyond the breakers, a distance of 50 to 75 yards or more. When the bait must be held in place you will need a heavy sinker to do the job and this type of weight requires a certain type of tackle.

The waves act continually on your line, first pulling down on it, and then releasing it as they break on the beach. The heavier the line and the rougher the sea, the more the waves will pull and the harder it will be to keep your bait secure on the bottom.

Obstructions that will cut or fray your line are found everywhere along the surf. Rocks, mussel beds, sod banks, and even the sand will present a constant hazard. Add to this the sharp teeth, rough hide, and razorlike gill plates and fins found on most saltwater fish and you begin to see why you need sturdy tackle to combat all these obstacles.

Sturdy does not necessarily mean heavy. There will be times and places where light tackle will be not only possible but desirable. The idea that a 14- or 15-foot rod, 30- or 40-pound line, and 6 ounces of weight must always be used to catch fish in the surf is simply not true. Certain conditions will make this super-heavy tackle necessary but there are also times when a one-handed spinning rod, 10-pound line, and a half-ounce jig will put more fish on the beach than you would ever catch with heavy tackle.

Quality, not size, is the key to success. The same elements that seek to destroy heavy tackle also work against the lighter stuff. If you go with high-quality products from the beginning and take care of your equipment it will serve you well.

Balance is another key factor in tackle selection. Most surf-fishing tackle is somewhat heavier in weight than tackle used in other types of fishing. If this weight is not properly balanced you will be uncomfortable with the tackle and soon tire of the sport. You must have balanced tackle to cast properly and to fight a big fish. If your tackle is unbalanced, your casting distance and accuracy will suffer; you will feel awkward and you won't be able to hold the rod properly, which will put your body out of balance as you try to compensate for the unbalance between rod and reel. This unbalance will tire you out more quickly than will the fish. You cannot land a trophy-sized bluefish, channel bass, or striper if you must spend more energy fighting the tackle than fighting the fish. I have seen more big fish lost to improper tackle than to any other factor.

Balance is critical between line size and sinker or lure weight as well. A heavy sinker cast on a light line will usually result in a break-off. On the other hand, a light lure cast with heavy line won't go very far.

There is one area of surf-fishing tackle where balance must be sacrificed to expediency. When you fish from the beach for small species such as croaker, king whiting, spot, or pompano it is often necessary to cast 4 to 5 ounces of sinker into a heavy surf. Under these conditions you will need tackle that is much heavier than the fish you are trying to catch. An 11-foot rod and a big surf reel filled with 17-pound-test line are heavy enough to land the biggest fish, but due to the weight of the sinker and the distance you must cast to reach smaller fish, heavy tackle is also required. This unbalance between tackle and fish removes some of the sport, but using tackle matched to the size of the fish would be impractical and unproductive.

Rods

The most specialized component in the surf fisherman's tackle arsenal is the surf rod. The length can be 10 to 14 feet or longer, and since most surf rods are designed to deliver the bait or lure over a long distance, they can become a bit unwieldy when you are fighting a big fish. As a comparison, an offshore trolling rod is designed to put maximum pressure on a fish during the fight but would be hard-pressed to cast a lure or bait beyond the breakers.

Surf rods vary not only in length but also in action. Each manufacturer has his own standard for grading rod blanks, but if you have a general idea of what type of action you are looking for the manufacturer's designation will be close enough for you to make a choice. The vast majority of surf rods on the market will be rated *medium* (1–3 ounces casting weight, 12–20-pound-test line), *medium heavy* (2–5 ounces casting weight, 15–25-pound-test line), or *heavy action* (3–6 ounces casting weight, 20–50-pound-test line).

With a choice as varied as this you need a good idea of exactly what you want before you enter the store. The only way to decide what type of rod suits your fishing style best is to try a variety of rods before you buy. The angler who contemplates surf fishing for the first time has a formidable task in selecting a rod. He must rely on the recommendations of others and should try out as many rods as he can before purchasing his own.

Length should be the first consideration. The most efficient cast will be made with a rod between 10 and 12 feet in length. What you must do is determine the length of rod that fits your size. You must not be overpowered by a rod that is too long or be unable to transfer your total casting power because your rod is too short. Many people believe the longer the rod is the longer the cast will be, but this simply is not true. A rod can only transfer power from the caster to the lure or sinker and a match must be made among all three factors.

Years ago I built a 14-foot rod with the idea that I could easily reach the outer bar with a tool of this size. I was wrong. The 14-footer was so long and unwieldy that my casting distance actually fell off. The only advantage of the big stick came from its ability to handle heavier weights. I was able to cast 8 ounces of lead and a big hunk of cut mullet to chopper bluefish during a northeast blow when anglers with shorter rods and lighter lines were unable to work with the extra weight. In a situation like that a 4- or 5-ounce sinker won't hold bottom and quickly washes back to the beach. The 14-foot rod did not deliver the bait any farther, but the fact that it could handle twice the weight of an 11- or 12-footer made it more practical on this occasion. The big rod currently resides in my basement and only sees action when conditions prevent the use of shorter rods.

Over the years I have found that an 11-foot spinning rod or a 10-foot casting rod that can handle 4 to 6 ounces of lead will serve the surf angler well in a variety of situations. A small man, a woman, or a young person might find a 10-foot spinning rod more comfortable, while an experienced surf caster who can use the extra length might choose a 12-foot rod. A 9-foot conventional rod can be used for casting plugs but is too short for bait fishing the high surf.

The material used to construct the rod can make a good deal of difference in the weight and casting ability of the finished product. Fiberglass and graphite are used by the major manufacturers and each has its own characteristics. Fiberglass rods are much more durable than graphite rods but they are also heavier and less sensitive. Graphite rods have a greater ability to transfer energy from the caster to the lure or sinker but there is a substantial difference in cost: the graphite rod will sell for much more than will one constructed of fiberglass.

The cost difference seems to be narrowing and with manufacturers using different amounts and types of graphite in their rods you can find reasonably priced products on today's market. I feel the advantages of a graphite rod's construction far outweigh those of a fiberglass rod and the difference in cost is justified. The novice surf caster should consider graphite because its lighter weight and better casting ability will help him learn the basics of the sport without becoming discouraged by awkwardness in the tackle.

There is some controversy over the efficiency of a two-piece rod as opposed to a one-piece rod. In the old days two-piece rods were held together by metal ferrules. These gadgets interfered with the action of the rod because they could not bend and acted like dampers between the two sections. Metal ferrules would also corrode and once this happened you were stuck with a one-piece rod that had the action of a two-piece rod.

The introduction of the fiberglass or graphite ferrule changed the situation and made a two-piece rod behave more like one constructed out of a one-piece blank. The new ferrules bend with the blank for an even transfer of energy during the cast. They maintain continuity of material all the way through the blank, which improves sensitivity over those joined by metal ferrules. While you can still end up with a ferrule that is difficult to separate, the prognosis is much better because the culprit is friction and not corrosion.

It is my opinion that the average surf caster would not be able to detect a difference between a one-piece rod and the two-piece rods on the market today. I fish with both types on a regular basis and both seem to work equally well. Unless you have a safe place to store and carry one-piece rods you will have no other choice than two-piece sticks. An 11- or 12-foot surf rod does not fit into the average car and it is also difficult to find storage space for it. This is especially true if your spouse doesn't share your love for surf fishing. A two-piece rod will fit into all but the smallest car and won't take up much space at home. You can even take it on a commercial airplane as carry-on luggage. As you can see, the two-piece rod is not only the most practical choice but is also as good a performer as its one-piece counterpart.

No rod is any better than the components used in its construction. This includes not only the type of material used to manufacture the blank but also the guides and the reel seat. Surf spinning rods should have a large gathering guide to keep the line from slapping against the blank during a cast. The next four or five guides should gradually taper down to the tip-top. I have seen slow-motion film showing how line behaves as it leaves a fixed-spool reel and travels through the guides. The circular spinning motion of the line all but disappears after it passes through the gathering guide. This guide should be just a bit smaller in diameter than the spool of the reel and should be supported well above the blank for maximum casting efficiency.

There are other surf fishermen who disagree with this theory. They believe aluminum oxide and other space-age materials used to construct modern guides reduce line friction to such an extent that the large stainless guides I use as gathering guides are unnecessary. Although the reduced friction is very important, I still maintain that keeping the line away from the blank will improve your casting distance.

The most efficient setup is one or two large stainless guides followed by a series of aluminum oxide guides and tip-top. The large gathering guide will aid in casting distance while the smooth, hard aluminum oxide guides will reduce line abrasion when you bring in a big fish or retrieve your lure or bait. The largest aluminum oxide guide on the market has a 50-millimeter outside diameter and the biggest stainless guide has a 75-millimeter outside diameter. Keep in mind that the inside diameter of these guides is going to be smaller than the outside diameter. With the stainless guide this difference is minimal, but with an aluminum oxide guide the difference can be considerable. Aluminum oxide guides have three components: a stainless brace, a rubber shock ring, and the aluminum oxide inner ring. Each of these decreases the inside diameter of the guide.

It may be difficult to find the perfect surf rod unless you build your own or have someone else build it for you. This will increase the cost substantially but will result in a rod that matches the owner's specifications. As a starting point, let me describe the two rods I have used for many years. Both are custom-built on fiberglass blanks, but if I were to have new ones made they would be on graphite.

The spinning rod is made from a medium-heavy 11½-foot blank. It has five guides and a tip-top. The spacing of the guides is 25 inches between the reel seat and the gathering guide, 26 inches to the second guide, 20 inches to the third, 15 inches to the fourth, 11 inches to the fifth, and 10 inches to the tip-top. The reel seat is 5 inches long and the butt of the rod is 22 inches from the base of the reel seat.

The conventional rod is 10 feet long and made from a heavy blank. The guide spacing is 33 inches from the reel seat to the first guide, 18 inches between the first and second guides, 14 inches to the third, 12 inches to the fourth, 12 inches to the fifth, and 7½ inches to the tip-top. All of these guides are aluminum oxide with heavy-duty braces for maximum support. The reel seat is 5 inches long and the butt is 26 inches from the end of the seat.

My favorite store-bought spinning rod is a two-piece blank made from a graphite composite. I find myself using this rod more and more because it is lighter than the one-piece fiberglass custom-made rod and it is easier to transport due to its two-piece construction. The gathering guide is 35 inches from the reel seat, the second guide is 24 inches from the first, the third is 19 inches, the fourth is 17 inches, the fifth is 13 inches, and the tip-top is 10 inches from the fifth guide. All of the guides are aluminum oxide but I use a reel that matches this rod and both are made by the same company. The gathering guide is a bit smaller than the reel face but is large enough to keep the line away from the blank when casting. The reel seat is 5 inches long and the base of the seat is 21 inches away from the butt.

A comparison of the two spinning rods reveals a longer butt section on the custom rod and a greater spacing between the reel seat and the gathering guide on the store-bought rod. I like a longer butt section for casting because the spread between my hands, with one on the end of the rod and the other on the reel, feels more comfortable. The longer spacing between the reel seat and the first guide on the manufactured rod is the result of a longer blank and a shorter butt section. This rod is not quite as comfortable for me to cast as is my custom rod but the difference is so slight and the graphite composite makes the rod so much lighter that I believe I can toss a bait or lure just as far with either rod.

Most reel seats are either stainless steel or graphite. Either of these materials will work well but the graphite seats are lighter and more comfortable to hold in cold weather. A graphite seat mounted on a graphite blank will provide the ultimate in sensitivity.

Grips are another component of a surf rod that requires serious consideration. The choice here will be between cork and *Hypalon,* a rubberlike material that is softer but less sensitive than cork. The butt sections of surf rods are too large in diameter for average-size cork rings so cork tape is used to make these grips. Some anglers tape the entire butt section and eliminate the reel seat. They use hose clamps to secure the reel to the blank and cover the reel seat and the area where it attaches to the rod with black electrical tape. This is a bit crude, but it's effective, especially when you are fishing in cold weather.

Hypalon grips are very comfortable to hold in all types of weather and you will find them on most manufactured surf rods. Many custom-rod builders use Hypalon grips not only because they are more comfortable than cork but because they look better, which can be important to someone who is spending several hundred dollars on a surf rod.

The selection of a surf rod always comes down to the preference of the surf caster. The specifications I have given are those I have found to be the best suited to my size and to the type of surf fishing I do. I believe similar types of rods would serve the vast majority of Atlantic Coast anglers in almost any of the varied types of surf conditions they are likely to encounter. Whether you choose to purchase a rod made by one of the many tackle manufacturers or have one built to your particular specifications, be certain the materials are of the highest quality and strength because the life of a surf rod is not easy and equipment not up to the task will fail.

Reels

A surf-fishing reel must be well built and it must have power. I doubt that there is any other type of fishing that puts a greater strain on a reel than does surf fishing. You will expect your reel to perform under the most difficult conditions. It must resist sand and saltwater spray as well as bouncing around in the car or on the front of a surf-fishing vehicle. It must aid you in casting long distances and be able to hold up while bringing a big fish to the beach. A poorly made reel will not survive and even a good reel will fail if you don't practice proper preventive maintenance.

At one time or another, I have seen just about every type of reel used on the beach. There are a few surf fishermen who depend on reels that were manufactured years ago and are no longer on the market. These people will go so far as having parts custom-made, at considerable expense, in order to maintain these reels. I met one surf fisherman from Long Island, New York, who designed and built his own reel. The finished product was not only a fine and sturdy fishing reel but also a work of art. Unfortunately, he only makes these reels for himself and even if he did make some for the market few of us could afford to buy them.

The most practical method for acquiring a surf reel is to buy one made by one of the many manufacturers in the fishing-reel market. As you glance through the catalogs or shop in your local tackle store you will see many reels that can be used for surf fishing, but some are better suited to the task than are others.

If we are looking for a reel to match our 11½-foot medium-heavy surf rod, we will need one that holds 300 to 350 yards of 17- to 20-pound-test monofilament line. The face of the reel should be close to the same diameter as the gathering guide, and the drag system should be very smooth and sealed as much as possible from sand and water.

You may think that 300 to 350 yards is a lot of line, but consider the conditions of surf casting. You will be tossing your bait or lure 75 to 150 yards into the ocean and probably walking another 25 to 50 yards away from the surf to stand on dry sand. This could add up to 200 yards of line from the rod tip to the bait. If you get lucky and hook a big channel bass, shark, or other trophy fish, it can easily take another 50 to 100 yards of line on the first run. Now you are down to 50 yards or less of line on the spool and a long job ahead getting the rest of the line and the fish back to the beach.

A full spool of line is essential for maximum casting efficiency. As the line leaves a fixed-spool reel it comes in contact with the outer lip of the spool. The more line that goes out, the more friction is created between the line and the lip as the outside diameter of the line on the spool diminishes. If you begin your cast with the spool half-filled with line, this friction will be much greater than with a completely filled spool.

In spite of the opinions of some surf fishermen, I believe the reels on today's market are far superior to those available in the past. Many of the new reels are made from graphite composites and other lightweight but very strong materials that resist the corrosion created by constant exposure to salt water. There are new drag systems made from materials that resist water and dissipate heat better than did previous components. There are even some spinning reels that feature the ability to free-spool line to a fish without opening the bail, and to apply full drag to set the hook by simply flipping a lever. Some of the newer reels have even eliminated the bail spring that has been a constant thorn in the side of surf casters because of its affinity for breaking at the most inopportune moments.

In an effort to overcome bail problems on surf spinning reels some anglers remove the bail and replace it with a manual pick-up. This is not a difficult task and some reel manufacturers supply the parts necessary for this conversion. If you can't find a kit to convert your spinning reel bail to manual pick-up you will have to do the job yourself or take the reel to a repair shop and have it done for you. The job is not too difficult. (But a good reel mechanic will probably do it better, quicker, and at such a reasonable price that you may not feel it is worth the aggravation to do it on your own.)

Simply remove the bail, cut away all but an inch or so above the roller, and replace this section on the reel. The hole where the other end of the bail used to fit should be filled with a nut and bolt to counterbalance the weight lost. I know there are many fishermen who get a lot of pleasure out of building or modifying their own equipment. I am not one of these fishermen. It has been my experience over many years that not only do experienced, professional reel mechanics and rod builders do a much better job than I do, but they do it quicker and they do it right the first time.

The roller on either a manual or an automatic bail must have a smooth surface and it must turn freely. This is the point where your line is under the most pressure and even the smallest nick or seizure on the roller as it turns can cause abrasion. Unlike fishing situations where you are casting only 20 or 30 feet, surf fishing requires a much longer cast

The proper way to hold a spinning reel.

and, consequently, you can ruin 200 yards of line very quickly if your roller is not functioning properly. If this happens you must fix the roller immediately and replace the entire spool of line.

Balance between rod and reel is critical. Nothing will decrease your casting distance and tire you out more quickly than an unbalanced outfit that is awkward to cast and to hold. When shopping for a reel, always mount it on the rod and check the balance. It should feel comfortable when held by the reel seat and should balance when placed on your hand within an inch or two of the point where the reel mounts to the rod. This balance can be fine-tuned by tapping lead strips to the butt of the rod.

Tackle companies that produce both rods and reels often recommend the best combination of their products for specific fishing situations. I have found these recommendations to be very good and if you follow them you should end up with a well-balanced outfit.

The choice of conventional reels for surf casting is not nearly as wide as is the selection of spinning reels. Spinning is preferred by most surf casters because it is easy to learn and works well in almost every surf-fishing situation. While conventional reels do require a bit more practice to master, the newer models with counterbalances and magnetic cast controls are much easier to operate than are those produced only a few years ago.

The advantage of a conventional revolving-spool reel over a spinning reel with a fixed spool is casting distance. The revolving spool stores casting energy and releases it during the cast, adding to the distance the lure or bait can travel. There is minimum friction as the line leaves the revolving spool because it is being thrown off as the spool turns. A fixed-spool reel remains stationary as the line is pulled from it by the energy created from the cast. The bait must push against the air and pull the line off the reel, which creates more drag and results in a shorter cast.

There are many other factors that control casting distance, but if all of these were equal the revolving spool would outcast the fixed. We will look into this aspect of surf fishing in a later chapter.

In the past, conventional reels were preferred by surf fishermen who went after big fish. This was due to the greater line capacity and better drag systems that were available only on large conventional reels. In today's market this is no longer the case because several manufacturers produce spinning reels that hold more than enough line to handle the biggest fish, and drag systems that will bring him to the beach.

The surf angler who plans to buy only one outfit should have no problem finding a spinning reel to fit his needs. Properly matched to a medium-heavy rod, this combination will allow him to fish anywhere along the Atlantic Coast with either bait or lures and have a reasonable chance for success.

Line

I have observed that the surf-fishing line preferred by most anglers is nylon monofilament. This is true for both spinning and conventional reels, and for good reason.

Monofilament line has the greatest abrasion resistance of any fishing line and is available in a wide variety of pound-test. Most surf-fishing situations require a line of 15- to 20-pound-test but many surf casters will use lines as light as 10- or 12-pound-test, with a shocker for greater casting distance.

The pound-test of the line is usually greater than the weight of the fish you will catch but any line lighter than 10 pounds will be very susceptible to abrasion or to breaking under the pressure of long-distance casting.

It is a good idea to employ a shock leader even when you use line between 15- and 20-pound-test. The shocker will take all the power you can put in the cast without snapping off and will give you a safety margin when you get your fish in close and want to put more pressure on to get him through the breakers. Another advantage to the shocker is a greater margin of abrasion resistance due to the increased diameter of the heavier line.

Your shock leader should be twice the pound-test of the running line. You will see some surf fishermen who use 50- or 60-pound shocker with 10- or 12-pound line, but most of these folks are more interested in casting distance than with catching fish.

A more practical approach would be a shock leader made from 40-pound line attached to a 17-pound running line. You may lose a few feet of casting distance, but this combination is much easier to work with and will hold a big fish much better than will the lighter running line. Do not use leader material to make your shocker. This line is much too stiff to lie on the reel and its thicker diameter will cut down your casting distance. It is also difficult to tie in a knot small enough to pass easily through the guides.

The length of the shocker should be 12 to 15 feet. This will allow your leader to lie one or two turns on the reel and still have enough length to let the bait or lure drop down to the gathering guide. Longer leaders can bind on the reel and shorter leaders leave the connecting knot between the reel and the tip-top, which can create problems during the cast. This knot is the weakest link in the shocker system because it will occasionally catch on a guide and break off. By having it on the reel spool at the start of the cast the knot will be traveling at maximum velocity when it gets to the guides, which will help push it safely through.

I have found the blood knot to be the best connection between shocker and running line. When properly tied it is shaped something like a barrel and passes as smoothly as possible through the guides. You can safely use the blood knot when the shock leader is no greater than twice the size of the running line.

Should you choose to use a heavier shock leader you will have to tie some different knots. Use a Bimini twist to double the standing line

Knots to Form Double-Line Leaders

The Bimini Twist creates a long length of doubled line that is stronger than the single strand of the standing line. It is most often used in offshore trolling, but is applicable in light tackle trolling in both fresh and salt water.

Measure a little more than twice the footage you'll want for the double-line leader. Bring end back to standing line and hold together. Rotate end of loop 20 times, putting twists in it.

Spread loop to force twists together about 10 inches below tag end. Step both feet through loop and bring it up around knees so pressure can be placed on column of twists by spreading knees apart.

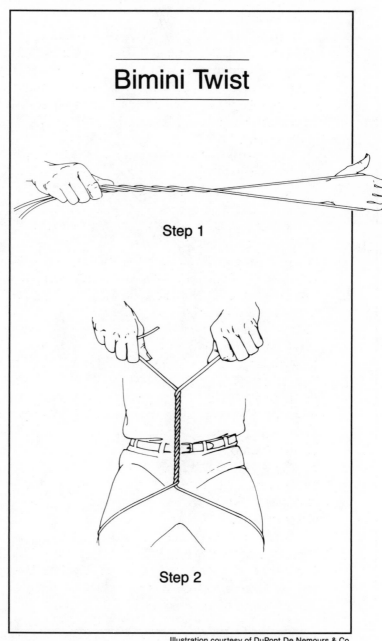

Bimini Twist

Step 1

Step 2

Illustration courtesy of DuPont De Nemours & Co.

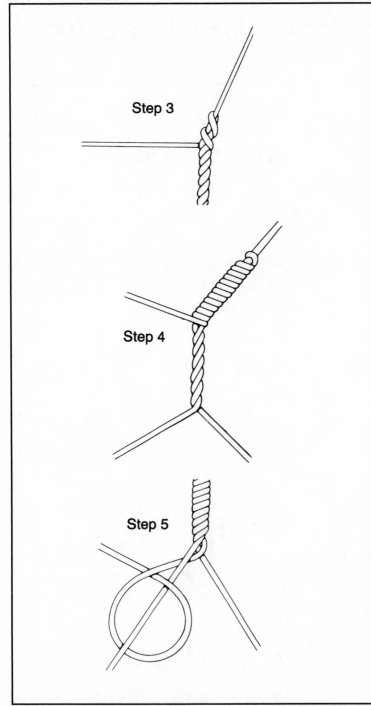

Step 3

With twists forced tightly together, hold standing line in one hand with tension just slightly off the vertical position. With other hand, move tag end to position at right angle to twists. Keeping tension on loop with knees, gradually ease tension of tag end so it will roll over the column of twists, beginning just below the upper twist.

Step 4

Spread legs apart slowly to maintain pressure on loop. Steer tag end into a tight spiral coil as it continues to roll over twisted line.

Step 5

When spiral of tag end has rolled over column of twists, continue keeping knee pressure on loop and move hand that has held standing line down to grasp knot. Place finger in crotch of line where loop joins knot to prevent slippage of last turn. Take half-hitch with tag end around nearest leg of loop and pull up tight.

Illustration courtesy of DuPont De Nemours & Co.

SURF FISHING THE ATLANTIC COAST

With half-hitch hold-
ing knot, release
knee pressure but
keep loop stretched
out tight. Using
remaining tag end,
take half-hitch
around both legs of
loop, but do not
pull tight.

Make two more
turns with the tag
end around both legs
of the loop, winding
inside the bend of
line formed by the
loose half-hitch and
toward the main
knot. Pull tag end
slowly, forcing the
three loops to gather
in a spiral.

When loops are
pulled up nearly
against main knot,
tighten to lock knot
in place. Trim end
about ¼ inch from
knot.
These directions
apply to tying
double-line leaders of
around 5 feet
or less. For longer
double-line sections,
two people may be
required to hold the
line and make initial
twists.

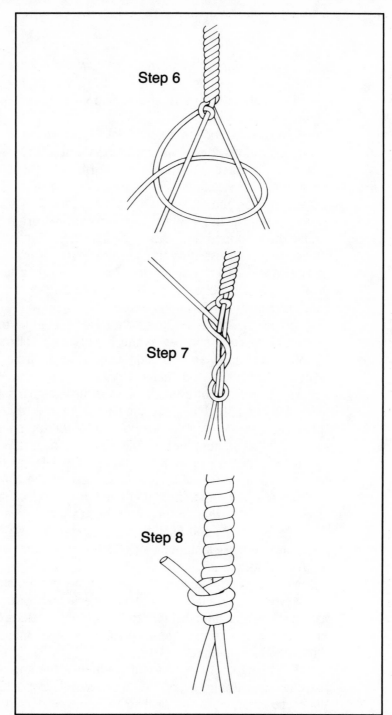

Illustration courtesy of DuPont De Nemours & Co.

and then an Albright knot with the heavy shock leader through the loop of the double line. This type of setup is generally used by tournament long-distance casters and is seldom required by actual fishing conditions.

One consideration you may want to give on shock leader length is the qualifications for an International Game Fish Association (IGFA) line-class world record. According to IGFA rules, the total leader length must not exceed 20 feet for line classes up to and including the 20-pound class, and 40 feet in line classes over 20 pounds. This technicality caused David Deuel's all-tackle record red drum to be registered under the 50-pound line class category rather than the 20-pound. Mr. Deuel caught his fish from the surf near Avon, North Carolina, using a heavy shock leader attached to 17-pound running line. Because the total length of the shocker was more than 20 feet the IGFA ruled the catch was made on 50-pound line.

Your choice of fishing line for the surf should be based on quality, not on price. Expect to pay as much as twenty dollars for a 600-yard spool; however, when you purchase top-grade fishing line you can expect long life and dependable service.

The properties of a quality line include high knot strength, thin diameter per pound-test, excellent abrasion resistance and limpness. The best lines compromise between all of these properties because to achieve the maximum for one will diminish the others somewhat.

For instance, if you want the thinnest possible line that will still test at 10 pounds, you will lose a good deal of the limpness, abrasion resistance, and knot strength you need in actual fishing situations. You can make a line that is very limp but this will severely reduce the abrasion resistance and knot strength. Everything must come together in balance to make a monofilament line that performs to the satisfaction of the surf fisherman.

No matter how good your line may be, it is no stronger than the knots you tie to attach it to your shock leader, lure, or bait. The connections you must be able to tie correctly include the blood knot, improved clinch knot, surgeon's loop, hook snell, Bimini twist, Albright knot, and the uni-knot.

The blood knot is used to join two lines, the improved clinch knot attaches your line to everything from swivels to hooks. The surgeon's loop and hook snell are used to make up leaders. The Bimini twist doubles your line, the Albright knot attaches a line to a loop, and the

Here is a system that uses one basic knot for a variety of applications. Developed by Vic Dunaway, author of numerous books on fishing and editor of "Florida Sportsman" magazine, the uni-knot can be varied to meet virtually every knot tying need in either fresh- or salt-water fishing.

Run line through eye of hook, swivel or lure at least 6 inches and fold to make two parallel lines. Bring end of line back in a circle toward hook or lure.

Make six turns with tag end around the double line and through the circle. Hold double line at point where it passes through eye and pull tag end to snug up turns.

Now pull standing line to slide knot up against eye.

Continue pulling until knot is tight. Trim tag end flush with closest coil of knot. Uni-knot will not slip.

THE UNI-KNOT SYSTEM

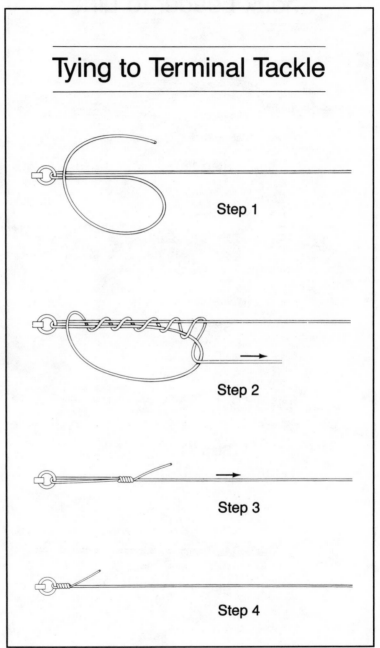

Tying to Terminal Tackle

Step 1

Step 2

Step 3

Step 4

Illustration courtesy of DuPont De Nemours & Co.

Shock Leader to Line

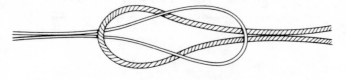

Step 1

When leader is five times or more the pound-test of line, double ends of both leader and line back about 6 inches. Slip loop of line through loop of leader far enough to permit tying uni-knot around both strands of leader.

Step 2

With doubled line, tie uni-knot around the two strands of leader. Use only four turns.

Step 3

Put finger through loop of line and grasp both tag end and standing line to pull knot snug around loop of leader.

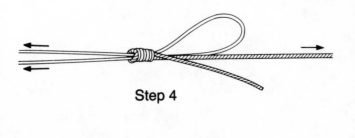

Step 4

With one hand pull standing leader (not both strands). With other hand pull both strands of line (see arrows). Pull slowly until knot slides to end of leader loop and all slippage is gone.

Illustration courtesy of DuPont De Nemours & Co.

Double Line Shock Leader

As a replacement for Bimini twist or spider hitch, first clip off amount of line needed for length of loop desired. Tie the two ends together with an overhand knot.

Step 1

Double end of standing line and overlap 6 inches with knotted end of loop piece. Tie uni-knot with tied loop around doubled standing line, making four turns.

Step 2

Now tie uni-knot with doubled standing line around loop piece. Again four turns.

Step 3

Hold both strands of doubled line in one hand, both strands of loop in other. Pull knots together until they barely touch.

Step 4

Tighten by pulling both strands of loop piece but only main strand of standing line (see arrows). Trim off both loop tag ends, which eliminate overhand knot.

Step 5

Illustration courtesy of DuPont De Nemours & Co.

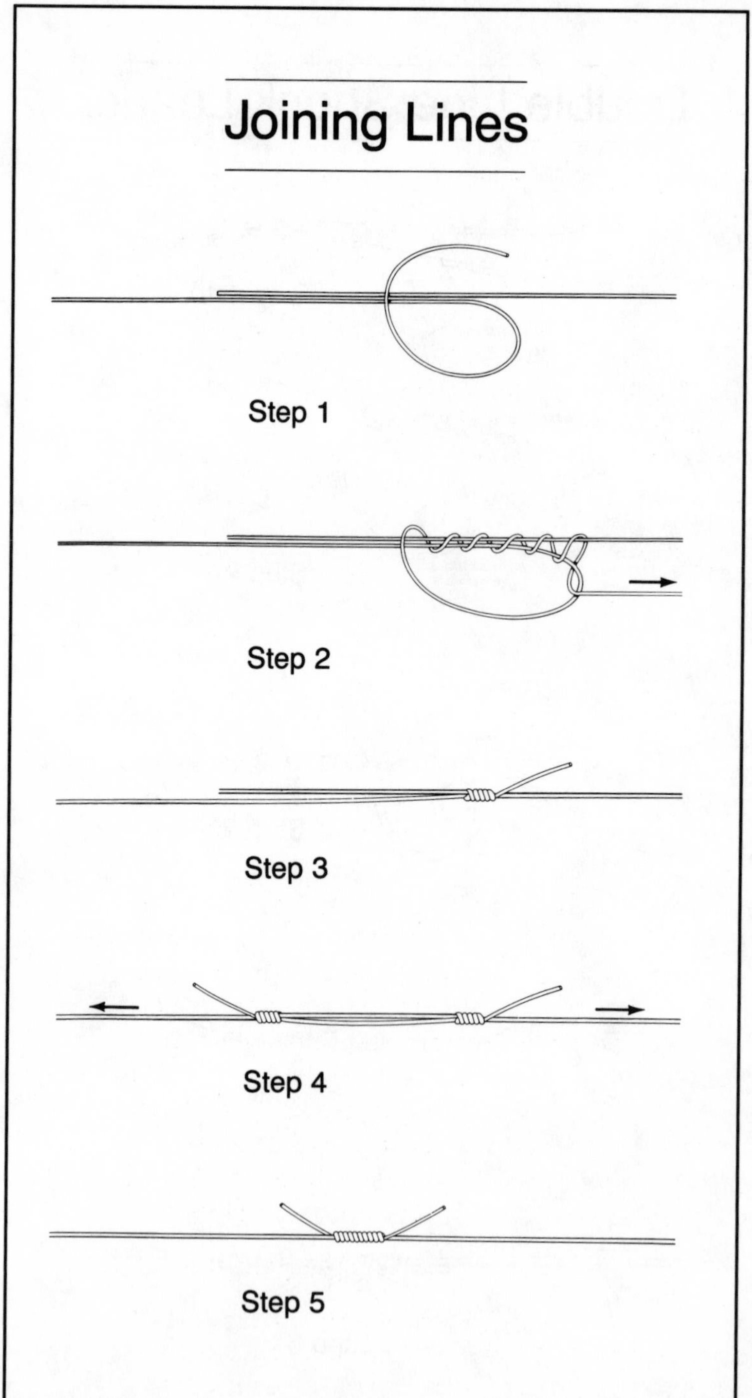

Joining Lines

Step 1

Overlap ends of two lines of about the same diameter for about 6 inches. With one end, form uni-knot circle, crossing the two lines about midway of overlapped distance.

Step 2

Tie uni-knot around leader with doubled line. Use only three turns and snug up.

Step 3

Pull tag end to snug knot tight around line.

Step 4

Pull knots together as tightly as possible and trim ends and loop.

Step 5

Pull the two standing lines in opposite directions to slide knots together. Pull as tight as possible and snip ends close to nearest coil.

Illustration courtesy of DuPont De Nemours & Co.

uni-knot system provides a method for using one basic knot in a variety of situations.

Practice is the only way to improve your knot-tying skills. The more times you tie a knot, the more efficient you will become at this chore.

Knots must never be jerked tight but, rather, pulled together with even but firm pressure. Wet line ties better than dry, so it is a good idea to moisten the knot with saliva or water before pulling it tight. Always trim off the tag end as close to the knot as possible without nicking the connection or cutting the running line. A properly tied knot will pass easily through the guides and will be less likely to attract weeds or other debris while in the water.

High-quality line combined with well-tied knots will allow you to get the most out of your tackle. The best baits or lures fished in the most productive waters will be useless if you can't get your catch back to the beach because your line broke or your knot failed.

Rigs

The rig you use to present your bait or lure to the fish is important for a variety of reasons. First, it should look as natural as possible. Second, it should help you set the hook and it must not fail as you work your catch back to the beach. Your rig is in direct contact not only with the fish but also with all the abrasive materials found on the ocean bottom. For this reason it must be strong but it must also be as inconspicuous as possible. As important as this piece of equipment is to your success in the surf it is seldom given much consideration by the average angler. This is one reason the average angler remains average.

A very basic surf rig is made up of a three-way swivel, a snelled hook, and a sinker snap. You simply loop the snelled hook through one eye of the three-way swivel, attach the sinker snap to the second eye, and tie your running line to the remaining eye of the swivel. With a variety of sinker weights and hook sizes you can quickly change your rig to match the size and type of fish available.

There are a wide variety of adornments you can place above your hook. A cork or Styrofoam float is often used to keep your bait above the bottom and away from hungry crabs. This method sounds better than it works. Crabs can easily swim up to grab your bait and will often destroy the float, which they hold in their claws while dining on

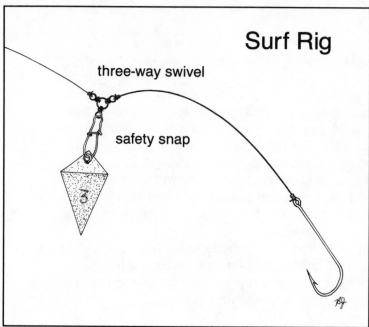

Surf Rig

three-way swivel

safety snap

Bob Jones illustration.

whatever delicacy you have chosen to serve them.

Bucktail hair will add to the attractiveness of a bait because it moves with the water to add lifelike motion to your otherwise dead presentation. The most common method of attaching this hair to your rig is tying it to a copper rivet and then sliding this down the leader to your hook. The hair is held on the rivet with thread, and a drop of epoxy over the thread will insure a secure connection. These bucktail teasers can be purchased in many tackle shops or you can make your own. The most popular colors are natural white, yellow, green, and red.

Red beads and spinner blades are also popular in some areas along the coast. The blades create motion and the beads act as bearings that allow the blades to spin without twisting the leader. This can be a very productive setup if you are casting and slowly retrieving a dead bait across the bottom. Summer flounder are one species that fall victim to this type of presentation.

Small rubber skirts placed ahead of the bait will move about in the current much like bucktail hair. Rubber does not move as easily as bucktail but it does impart its own action, which can be attractive to various fish.

You should keep one fact in mind when adorning your dead bait. Fish have a very acute sense of hearing. They can detect vibrations in the water and quickly home in on the origin of the sound. Any mechanism that creates a sound similar to the sounds made by the fish's natural food will attract his attention. While bucktail hair, spinner blades, beads, rubber skirts, and other dressings look good to the fisherman, they *sound* good to the fish. It is this sound that attracts them long before they ever see the bait. The odor of the bait is another attraction and the combination of the two act together to convince the fish he should eat your offering.

Hook style and size are determined by the type of fish you are trying to catch. One mistake made by many anglers is using a hook that is too small. While it is possible to use a hook that won't fit inside a fish's mouth, it is not likely. I have seen northern kingfish, who have relatively small mouths, caught on 5/0 and larger hooks intended for channel bass. I do not suggest that you should fish for kingfish with a 5/0 hook, but don't be afraid to use a 1/0 Chestertown when after these bottom feeders.

The problem with small hooks is their inability to hold the fish as you try to bring it back to the beach. They may not be big enough to penetrate completely through the mouth, so the barb cannot do its job. Also, small hooks are made from thin wire, which will straighten out under pressure.

The largest bluefish I have ever taken from the surf weighed 18 pounds and was caught at Pea Island, just south of Oregon Inlet, North Carolina. I was using a 5/0 stainless steel O'Shaughnessy hook on a 10-inch wire leader. The fish hit a chunk of cut mullet and immediately peeled off 40 yards or more of line against a very firm drag. He jumped clear of the water three or four times and after a solid ten-minute battle I finally beached him. The hook was bent completely out of shape, the float was broken in half, and the sinker snap was mangled to such a degree that the sinker and the slide that holds the snap shut had disappeared. This was a brand-new rig made from the finest material available, but one big bluefish had destroyed it. A rig made from inferior materials or a smaller hook size would have allowed this trophy to escape.

Monofilament leaders will work in most situations, but when you are after big bluefish or sharks you must use a wire leader ahead of the hook. Both of these species tend to swallow a bait, hook and all, and this will allow the leader to come in contact with their very sharp teeth. It doesn't take much imagination to foresee the consequences of

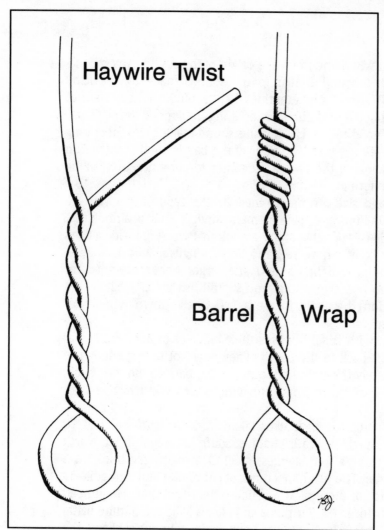

Haywire Twist

Barrel Wrap

Bob Jones illustration.

this encounter if the leader is anything but wire. Single-strand wire will do the job but I have found braided wire is easier to work with and will resist the kinking that results in the failure of single-strand wire leaders.

To make a leader from single-strand wire you must use the Haywire twist to form a loop in one end and to attach the hook to the other end. When making a Haywire twist you must lay the wire over itself much like a braided pigtail. Simply laying the tag end over the standing wire and not twisting the two together will result in slippage under pressure and the leader will be likely to fail. Finish your Haywire twist with a barrel wrap, and then break, do not cut, the tag end off as close to the standing wire as possible.

Braided wire is much easier to use because you do not have to tie a twist or any other knots. Simply form a loop by using the metal sleeves designed for this purpose and sized to fit the braided wire you are using. I have found 20-pound braided wire works well for blues up to 10 pounds, but I switch to 40-pound braided wire leader when the big choppers move in during the spring and fall. When you are in doubt it is better to use the heavier leader than to lose a big fish.

You can attach the metal sleeves to the leader with fishing pliers but you will get better results by using the tool designed for this specific task. Berkley makes a special set of crimping pliers for use with their braided wire leader and sleeves. High Seas also makes a fine crimping tool that is used for the heavier braided wire or cable leaders.

It has been my experience that wire leaders of less than 12 inches work best in the surf. Longer leaders tend to wrap around the standing line and when a fish hits the bait it will pull against the line with the wire leader causing a break-off. Shorter, stiffer leaders prevent this type of mishap.

Although I use a single-hook rig for at least ninety percent of my surf fishing, there are times when a two-hook rig will produce better action. You may hear these referred to as top-bottom rigs but this is not an accurate description when applied to surf fishing.

Consider a two-hook rig with the leaders spaced 10 to 12 inches apart. If you have cast this combination out 50 to 100 yards from shore, the angle of the line will be almost parallel to the bottom by the time you reach the rig. This will result in both hooks being on the bottom, unless you float one and weight the other. Even the floated hook will not rise more than the leader length off the bottom, which in most cases will result in a two-hook bottom rig and not a top-bottom rig, which would more aptly describe the same setup when fished vertically from a boat or pier.

The two-hook rig is employed when small fish such as spot, croaker, kingfish, or snapper blues are the target. The two-hook rig will let you catch two of these little critters per cast, thereby improving the efficiency of your efforts. Two baits will also give you a second chance to hook one of these smaller fish, who can quickly strip a bait without getting caught.

No one should be so greedy as to use a two-hook rig when chopper

Two-hook Rig

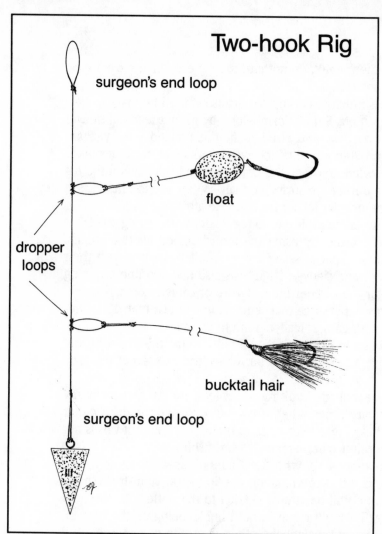

surgeon's end loop

float

dropper
loops

bucktail hair

surgeon's end loop

Bob Jones illustration.

blues, big red drum, or other trophy fish are in the surf. Hooking two of these tackle busters would not be difficult, but getting both of them back to the beach could prove to be a very unpleasant task. Stick to a single-hook rig for the bigger fish and double up only on the little guys.

I fashion my double-hook rigs out of 40-pound leader material. I do not use any hardware such as snaps, swivels, or standoffs. This keeps the cost of the rig down and makes it less obvious in the water.

You will use two knots to tie your rig. A surgeon's loop is made on each end of the leader and two dropper loops are spaced between. The total length of the finished leader will be 12 to 18 inches, so you should begin with a 20- to 24-inch section of line. I tie the bottom dropper loop about 2 inches above the sinker loop and the top dropper is 3 to 5 inches below the surgeon's loop that is used to connect the rig to the standing line. I have found that a swivel snap tied to the standing line with an improved clinch knot makes this a better connection than tying the line directly to the leader. The swivel snap also takes up the twisting motion of the rig as you crank it in, which normally would put a twist in your line, and a twisted line will cause you many problems.

Another rig that finds favor among surf casters is the fish-finder. It is so named because the line can move without carrying the sinker and in certain applications you can move the bait along the bottom to find the fish. In the surf this is not the primary use of the fish-finder rig. Rather, it is used to allow a fish to move off with the bait without feeling the pressure of the sinker. Your quarry then has time to mouth or turn the bait and swallow it before you try to set the hook.

The fish-finder rig requires some sort of mechanism that will allow the standing line to pass through without carrying the sinker along. The most efficient of these devices is a small nylon sleeve attached to a sinker snap. The standing line is passed through the sleeve before the leader and hook are attached. Once again, it is best to use a swivel snap between the line and leader because a knot could become jammed in the sleeve, defeating the purpose of the rig.

Channel bass are one species of fish that usually requires some time between the pick-up of the bait and the snelling of the hook. The fish-finder rig is ideal for catching these fish, but because the sinker slides up and down the line, casting distance can be adversely affected. Several variations on the fish-finder rig have been developed in an attempt to overcome this problem. One such rig uses a very short leader, 6 inches or less, while another variation uses a longer leader, up to 3 feet, but the sinker movement is restricted to the length of the leader.

The short-leader method works by keeping the action between the bait, which is usually quite large, and the sinker, to a minimum. When you cast these two heavy, large objects, the big bait and the sinker, they usually oppose each other and the resulting wind resistance will work to separate them, as well as hold down your casting distance. The short leader keeps the bait and the sinker close together so that they travel as one unit through the air.

If you want to use a longer leader, you can place a metal crimp

A fish-finder rig used for red drum.

about 6 inches above the hook, slide the leader through the fish-finder, and tie your loop about 3 feet above the crimp. You have combined the advantage of a short leader from the sinker to the bait but still have 3 feet of leader to the line, which can be important in taking up the abrasion from the tough scales of a channel bass or the rough bottom where he is often found.

Another variation on this idea is to use a short leader in combination with a shocker. Most channel-bass fishermen use 20-pound running line, so the shocker would be 40-pound line, and this should be sufficient to take most of the abuse. Leaders are generally made from 50- to 70-pound material.

Fish-finders should not be used when you are trying to catch big bluefish. Blues do not need time to swallow a bait and the sliding sinker will often work the hook out of a blue's mouth, especially if he makes a few jumps. I generally save my fish-finder rigs for drum, big weakfish, and sharks.

As you move up and down the Atlantic Coast you will find a variety of rigs on tackle-shop shelves. They will be called by many names and some people will try to convince you that only one specific rig will work in that particular area. If you examine these rigs you will find they all fit into the three categories we have discussed: single hook, double hook, or fish-finder. In certain areas a particular color or hook style may be more effective due to the clarity of water, color of the bottom, or

SURF FISHING THE ATLANTIC COAST

type of bait used, but the actual construction of the rig will not vary a great deal.

Try to avoid any type of wire rig unless you are after toothy critters. Make up your own rigs and snell your own hook to save money and to be sure you have the exact style and type of rig and hook you wish to use. When you buy a rig check the material and the knots to be sure you have a quality product. Attention to detail can make the difference between catching fish and hauling water.

Hooks

When it comes to fishing tackle, hooks are the bottom line. There are many styles of hooks on the market and some have specific uses, but the surf fisherman need only concern himself with a few styles and sizes.

Select your hooks to fit the size of the fish you are trying to catch; if you are unsure, go to a bigger size. Even the small surf species can be caught on at least a 1/0 size hook. This includes king whiting, spot, and pompano.

The type of bait you plan to use will also affect the style and size of your hook. Long thin baits such as bloodworms require long thin hooks such as Chestertowns or Carlisles. Big chunky baits work best with O'Shaughnessy or Mustad-Beak hooks. I have been using the wide-gap or English-style hooks for flounder and weakfish with good success over the past few years. I am also quite pleased with the results I have had using Tru-Turn hooks in their saltwater or Sea Perior styles.

You must be certain that the hooks you select are designed for saltwater use. Freshwater hooks are not made to withstand the corrosion imposed by salt water. They will catch fish in salt water but they won't last very long. Saltwater hooks are not only resistant to corrosion, but they are also stronger than comparable hooks used in fresh water. A hook that would safely hold a 10-pound largemouth bass would soon be destroyed in the jaws of a 10-pound bluefish.

The major hook manufacturers will indicate if their products are made for salt water or fresh. Mustad, Eagle Claw, and Tru-Turn all produce quality products that will withstand the rigors of surf fishing.

No matter how well a hook is made, it will still require sharpening before it is ready for use. The smaller hooks can be touched up with a hook sharpening stone, while the larger sizes may require the use of a file or a larger stone.

Always inspect the point of the hook for damage after each fish is taken or if the hook becomes fouled on the bottom. A hook with a broken or bent point will not catch fish.

Select hooks with a bent-up eye if you plan to snell them to a monofilament leader. Straight-eye hooks work best with a wire leader.

There is one type of hook I have used successfully in a number of applications: it is the Mustad Ryder-style #92586 hollow-point beak hook. Available in sizes 1/0 to 5/0, these hooks have a long shank with a small "ryder" or bait-holding hook soldered near the eye. I use them with whole-finger mullet or spot as well as with strips of baitfish or squid to catch everything from bluefish to flounder. They are particularly effective on short strikers, such as blues, because the larger hook is in the rear of the bait.

Sinkers

Most sinkers used in surf fishing are designed to hold your bait in one location against the forces of wind, wave, and current. They have a triangular shape with the eye at the top of the pyramid. The pointed end sinks into the sand until the flat end is covered. This digging-in action helps to hold the rig in one place. The flat top of a pyramid sinker will also dig into the sand as you crank your bait back to the beach. This imparts a grab-and-release action that is sometimes confused with a fish strike until the angler becomes accustomed to it.

There are some variations to the standard pyramid sinker that have found favor with surf fishermen along the Atlantic Coast. The first is known as the *hurricane sinker.* It is shaped like a bullet instead of a pyramid, but the top is flat with a triangular shape. The smooth surface on the leading edge of the hurricane sinker is supposed to give you better casting efficiency, while the flat triangle top still digs into the sand.

British surf casters who come to the United States have brought along their own brand of sinker. These are pointed at both ends to present an aerodynamic surface to the wind when casting. They use wires passed through the bottom of the sinker to dig into the sand and hold bottom. The wires trip backward when you pull the rig out of the sand and you can crank your fish or bait back in without undue resistance.

I have used all three types of sinkers and have found the standard pyramid to be equal in effectiveness to the hurricane style. If there is any major difference between the two as far as casting distance or holding ability, I have not been able to find it.

The British-style sinker with the wires is adequate but I have used it on only a few occasions. It probably does improve your casting distance a bit, but keep in mind that English anglers don't use the same rigs and baits as we Americans do. They have a very gradual beach and must cast a long distance to reach productive water. Their rigs employ smaller hooks and baits, which do not have as much wind resistance as a big chunk of mullet or a live spot. I am sure the shape of the sinker is much more critical to this type of fishing and casting than it is to our situation in this country.

Along the Atlantic Coast it may be important to get your bait out a ways, but it is just as important to make sure it stays there until you desire to bring it in. A 4-ounce hurricane sinker buried in the sand will be considerably more difficult to dislodge than will the same-size British sinker with only two thin wires to hold it in place.

There are times when you don't want your bait to stay in one place. Flounder fishermen like to keep their offering on the move because the flounder tend to stay in one place and let the food come to them. In these situations a *bank sinker* is the perfect solution. It is shaped somewhat like a teardrop and will move easily along the bottom. Bank sinkers will also work well in places where the bottom is plagued with obstructions. Rocks, stumps, weeds, sod banks, and other structure will often hold fish but will also hold on to your sinker. Pyramid or hurricane sinkers seldom return from a trip through this type of terrain and you will lose your share of rigs even with the smooth bank style, but you will also get more of them back.

If the bottom is particularly treacherous, you can tie the sinker to the rig with a lighter monofilament, using an overhead knot. The combination of the lighter line and the weak knot will allow the sinker to break off without taking the entire rig with it. A hooked fish can also hang up your sinker, so the break-away line may also help you get your catch to the beach.

If you plan to make your own sinkers you will find molds available for pyramid and bank sinkers but may encounter some difficulty locating molds for hurricane or British styles. If you insist on making these styles you will probably end up making the molds as well.

Snaps and Swivels

I recommend a ball-bearing snap swivel at the end of your line when you are fishing the surf. This piece of equipment has two advantages: first it allows you to change your rig without retying any knots; second it helps to keep your line from twisting. The first is only a convenience, the second is a necessity.

Line does not twist by itself, it has to be twisted by something. This happens when the rig or lure spins as you crank it in or if you crank against the drag with a spinning reel. Once the line is twisted it will act like a giant slinky and you will not be a happy angler.

A quality ball-bearing swivel is the best insurance you can have against line twist. It should be matched to a quality snap that exceeds the line test by at least two times. I use an improved clinch knot to attach the line to the snap swivel.

While it is good to use a snap swivel of 60- to 100-pound-test, you can overdo this and use one that is too big for the job. Keep in mind that the snap swivel is going to create drag in the air when you cast and resistance to the water as you fish. The smaller snap swivels will hold any fish you are likely to catch while presenting less resistance to the wind and water.

The snap is just as important as the swivel. I strongly recommend the Coastlock, or Duo-Lock snaps. All are made from one piece of stainless-steel wire and in many years of use I have not experienced a failure with either of these products.

As with most other types of fishing equipment there are less expensive types of swivels and snaps on the market. If you choose economy over quality you will save some money but I promise you will lose some fish, and you may be assured that the fish you lose will not be the little ones.

Artificial Lures

Many surf fishermen believe there is a certain mystique surrounding the use of artificial lures. Those who use them feel they are superior while bait fishermen may believe lures are ineffective or too difficult to use. Both schools of thought are incorrect.

The selection and presentation of the proper lure is no more difficult than the selection and presentation of the proper bait. There are times and locations when lures produce better results than baits and there are other circumstances when baits will outproduce lures. The complete surf angler will be able to make the proper choice and will not be swayed by preconceived notions about which fishing method carries the greatest influence.

Swimming Plugs

Surf-fishing plugs were originally larger versions of freshwater plugs. The first two people to create and market plugs designed specifically for saltwater use were Stan Gibbs and Bob Pond. Both of these men fished the same waters for the same species, primarily striped bass, but their creations look entirely different.

The original Bob Pond Atom plug was made from wood and used a metal lip to provide swimming action. It had a body shaped somewhat like a fish, with a blunt head, rounded body, and a tail that tapered back to a point. The Gibbs plug was made entirely from wood, including the swimming lip. It was shaped like a milk bottle, with a large head, thin neck, and rounded body.

Both lures employ treble hooks and a heavy metal wire that runs through the body to connect the hooks to the eye. This wire is necessary to resist the powerful pressure that a big blue or striper can enforce on a lure. Hooks that are simply screwed on to a plug's body can be torn off.

Bob Pond currently produces his original models but uses plastic molding to construct them. The Gibbs plugs are still made from wood. Many other companies have made saltwater plugs since Pond and Gibbs introduced the first models. A few of these other companies are still in business, but many others have fallen along the seaside. I think it is a considerable tribute to the pioneers of plug casting in the surf that their original inventions have survived the great changes in fishing tackle, technique, and fish population that have occurred during the forty or more years since these plugs were introduced.

When compared to the variety of plugs available in the freshwater market, the selection for saltwater anglers is relatively small. Narrowing this selection down to those plugs suitable for surf fishing leaves only a few that will produce on a regular basis.

A surf-fishing plug must be heavy enough and have the proper shape for efficient casting. It must have a design that imitates the swimming action of a baitfish and makes this imitation appealing to the game fish you are trying to catch. As an example, if the striped bass are feeding on mackerel and your plug imitates the action of a bunker, it may be ignored. On the other hand, if bluefish are smashing schools of bunker and your plug imitates a mackerel, the blues will probably gobble it up without hesitation. Even in this situation it is better to use a plug that resembles the current prey because even bluefish will occasionally become selective about their feed.

Some of the hollow plastic plugs, such as the Cotton Cordell swimmers, can be loaded with mineral oil or water to add weight and thereby increase casting distance. The extra weight will dampen the action of the plug, but this is seldom a problem because the slower action is usually more attractive to game fish such as weakfish and striped bass.

Some other name brand plugs that do well in the surf are Rebel, Bommer, Creek Chub, Bagley's, and Storm. Rapala produces a wooden plug that can be quite effective in quiet water.

When selecting a surf plug you should be sure the product will hold up under the rigorous conditions of saltwater fishing. The hooks must be strong, with stainless steel or nickel alloy the best choice. Examine the method used to attach the hook to the lure. If it is not securely fastened by a through-wire connection you may have to modify the plug before it will hold up to big saltwater fish.

Some plugs use an eye ring that is screwed or molded into the body. A split ring is attached to the eye and this connects the hook. If the screw eye is molded into the plastic it will have a strong base, but if it is screwed in it can work itself out. Putting a small amount of epoxy at the junction of the screw eye and the plug can strengthen this connection.

Most saltwater plugs come equipped with three sets of treble hooks. These hooks not only increase your chances of hooking a fish but also produce the exact action the manufacturer was trying to achieve.

Weakfish tend to hit a plug in the middle. Striped bass are head hunters and bluefish usually hit the back end of a bait. Since you can seldom choose exactly which type of fish you are going to catch, it is a good idea to leave all three sets of treble hooks installed.

One exception to this is the bluefish. These creatures cause so much commotion when they are landed that the unused trebles become lethal weapons. When the blues are feeding it is unlikely that you will find too many other fish in the neighborhood. For this reason many surf casters prepare a few plugs with a single hook on the tail and often remove the other two trebles. This will create a very lively plug, which bluefish like, and it gives you six fewer hook points to worry about as you try to remove the blue from the plug.

The swimming action of a plug is usually determined by the lip on the front. Some plugs, such as the Gibbs Darter, do not have a lip, but the front half of the plug is angled to give a very enticing action as it works through a rip or is slowly cranked back to the beach.

Large, long lips will cause a plug to dive for the bottom. This may be desirable for those who troll from a boat but seldom gives good results from the beach. The deep diver, when worked on the almost parallel angle of surf fishing, goes down to the bottom and drags along in the sand. In the wash it creates extreme pressure on the line and can be very difficult to move. If there are any obstructions on the bottom your plug will surely be lost.

Keep the lip size on your surf plug in the shallow to medium-depth size. This will keep the plug working somewhere between the surface and the bottom without hanging up.

Plugs will take fish during broad daylight, but they are most effective at night or during the times of twilight or dawn. These are the times when fish generally move into the shallow waters of the surf and this is when they tend to feed at mid-water levels or on the surface.

A fish has excellent night vision and can easily find a swimming plug even when the sky is so dark we cannot see any light at all. If a fish looks up toward the surface on a dark night, he will see your plug silhouetted against the sky because the extremely sensitive rods in his eyes move to the front after dark and they detect even the slightest amount of light. This is why a fish will hit a black lure at night but may not be able to find it as well in the daylight; because the rods in his eyes are no longer predominant and the cones do not pick out contrast as well.

Color selection is important when choosing which plug to use, but keep in mind that a fish cannot see color, only contrast. He is aware of the shade and size of the local baitfish so this should be a starting point when selecting plug color and size. Pick out some plugs that are shaped like your local baits and purchase them in several colors and sizes. Use the dark plugs on dark days and bright plugs on bright days and if that doesn't work, switch them around until something produces a strike.

To properly work a plug you must be aware of the wave action. A lure tossed in front of a breaker will be tossed about in the wash and will never have a chance to work properly. Watch the waves before you cast and place the plug in the clean water behind the breakers. Work it back to the beach in this area, adjusting the speed to keep it ahead of the next breaking wave.

Placing and working a plug properly requires some practice and experience, especially on a dark rainy night when the breakers look like thin white lines on the horizon. Start your plug casting during the daytime. You probably won't catch too many fish, but you will develop a rhythm with the waves. As you become more accustomed to plug casting you can begin to work at night. It does not take as long as you might expect before you will be proficient in placing the plug perfectly on almost every cast.

More so than any other type of fisherman, the plug caster works the tides. He must exert a great deal of energy casting and retrieving his lure hour after hour, so he wants to be sure his efforts are not wasted at times when the fish are unlikely to feed.

Each piece of beach has its rips, sloughs, bars, and rocks that occur only during certain periods of the tide. The plug caster must know which piece of beach is likely to produce at what stage of the tide and then he must be there when the tide is right.

It has been my experience that the tide is never right during the day and is only right at the most inconvenient times during the night. The hours between 2:00 and 4:00 A.M., when it is too late to stay up and too early to get up, are generally favored by the tides. This is the reason plug casters may seem a little strange when compared to other surf fishers, who keep more civilized hours.

Those who plan to do a lot of plug casting may want to select some specialized tackle. A graphite rod is very helpful because of its lighter weight and improved sensitivity. Consider that a plug fisher will make more casts in a week than a bait fisher will make all season and you can see why the light weight is important.

Sensitivity is necessary because some fish don't hit a plug with the same force they hit a bait. Weakfish seem to swim up and engulf the plug and may move toward the angler, which makes the strike difficult to detect. Striped bass usually tap the plug once or twice before taking it and you must be able to feel the taps so that you can prepare for the strike.

Poppers

A popping plug works across the surface of the water, creating a commotion that attracts fish. Poppers are used almost exclusively during the day and they provide some of the most exciting action you will find in any type of fishing.

The three most popular poppers are made by Gibbs, Atom, and Creek Chub. The Gibbs model is known as the Polaris and has a big head, thin neck, and a bottle-shaped body. It will float at rest and can be worked slowly with pauses that will often encourage a fish to strike. The Atom Striper Swiper and Creek Chub poppers do not float at rest. They are worked in a fairly rapid movement and should imitate a baitfish fleeing from a predator.

The Creek Chub and Atom models are heavier and have a more aerodynamic shape than does the Gibbs lure. This gives them better casting performance, especially if there is a wind blowing that could divert a lighter lure.

Another style of surface lure that is especially effective on bluefish is the pencil popper. One model is made by Gibbs and another by Cotton Cordell. Both are shaped like a long drop of water and weighted in the stern to sit tail-down when at rest. The weight in the back also helps the angler cast this plug. It takes a bit of practice to operate this lure. First you must cast it out, then remove all slack from the line. Next, place the butt of the rod between your legs and begin to reel in the lure very slowly. As you work the plug back to the beach you must whip the rod tip up and down as fast as possible. This is sort of like walking and chewing gum at the same time. You are cranking the plug in with one hand and whipping the rod up and down with the other. I find a spinning reel and matching rod work best for this type of action. All of this work is transferred to the plug and it jumps out of the water in the same manner as a school of baitfish. When properly operated, the pencil popper will entice a strike when all other methods have failed.

Several years ago there was quite an interest in a surface lure known as the Nantucket Ballistic Plug. It looks like a whiskey bottle with a treble hook on the bottom. The model I have was made by Nantucket Ocean Products and called the *BB75 Bullet*. Besides being shaped to resist the wind, this plug was also quite heavy. It used four or five egg sinkers as ballast and they added to the plug's action by rolling around inside and creating noise. As is the case with many good fishing plugs, the Nantucket Ballistic is no longer manufactured. Some anglers still make their own and you may find homemade models on the shelves of some tackle shops along with other lures that are out of production.

Companies such as Rebel, Cotton Cordell, and Arbogast also make poppers that will work in the surf. Most of these lures are not heavy enough to cast into a wind, but if the weather is calm and the fish are close to the beach they will do an admirable job.

Because poppers require a bit of hard work to produce the proper action, most surf fishermen do not use them unless they are reasonably sure there are fish in the area. Tossing and retrieving a slow-swimming plug can be a relaxing form of fishing but making a big popper splash across the surface of the ocean for an hour or two will tire the most ardent angler.

Poppers will work at times when swimming plugs have failed to produce a strike. Fish are competitive creatures and if they think a meal is getting away they will often take up the chase.

While almost all of the larger game fish will occasionally feed on the surface, you will find such species as bluefish and striped bass most susceptible to a popper. Blues are pelagic fish, which means they inhabit the surface of the sea, so they are particularly fond of munching on bait as it frantically tries to jump out or swim across the top of the water. Stripers will feed on top, especially when they move into the shallow water of the surf. I have seen times when both of these species had bait cornered in the wash and every cast produced a savage surface strike from one or the other.

Because it is so visible, I find surface plugging to be one of the most exciting forms of surf fishing. When a big blue pounces on a popper the surface explodes in white foam and it feels as if your arms have been jerked out of your shoulders. The blue will generally stay on top, giving you several more jumps before you can drag him from the wash. After two or three of these bouts most of us are ready for something cold to drink and a place to rest.

Rigging Plugs

You can simply tie a plug to the end of your line, toss it into the surf, and retrieve it back in, but you probably won't be satisfied with the results of this rigging method.

First of all, plugs need freedom of movement. If you tie the line to the eye of the plug it will dampen the action. Second, a plug fisherman will cast many more times per hour than will a bait fisherman. For this reason you will need a shocker on your line to take the added abuse it will receive from so many casts. Finally, you should use a fairly heavy leader between the shocker and the plug. Most of the abrasions, either from the fish's teeth, gill plates, scales, or fins will be directed at this section of your line, and if it fails you will lose not only the fish but an expensive plug as well.

I make my leaders from 40- to 60-pound monofilament leader material. Each is a simple affair with a swivel tied to one end and a Coastlock or Duo-Lock snap on the other. The finished length of the leader will be approximately 2 feet. You don't want it any longer or the swivel would come in contact with the tip of the rod, and anything much shorter will not serve the purpose.

You can tie a surgeon's loop in each end of the leader and thread the snap and swivel through the loop, but this will apply additional drag in the water and could cause the plug to operate improperly. A better system would employ a palomar or improved clinch knot to hold the snap and swivel.

A ball-bearing swivel is always the best choice to prevent line twist, but I have used the less expensive barrel swivels with good success. The color choice for both swivels and for snaps should be black. Shiny terminal gear can cause problems because some fish will hit the swivel while others may be spooked by it.

In some areas of the East Coast a dropper may be added ahead of the plug. I have used big flies, small rubber swimming lures, and small bucktails as a dropper with most of my success coming on the fly. These flies are tied on 4/0 or larger stainless hooks. They are not particularly complicated and may only be a few feathers tied to the hook and sealed on with a drop of epoxy.

The object of this system is to imitate a baitfish: the dropper is fleeing from a predator, the plug. In most instances the game fish will hit the dropper. We suspect this attack is a response to the competitive

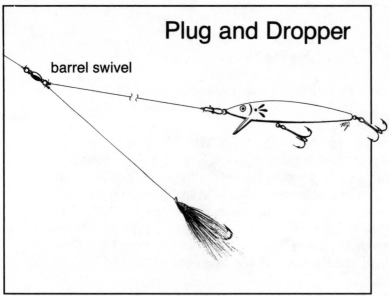

Plug and Dropper

barrel swivel

Bob Jones illustration.

nature of the fish, who wants to win the bait away from the other predator.

Droppers will work in front of swimmers or poppers but seem to be most effective with slow-moving swimming plugs. They may also be used with metal lures, which can be cast into a wind much easier than can a plug.

You will have to modify your leader if you plan to use a dropper. I tie a second leader line off of the swivel and attach this to the dropper. Use good stiff leader material and keep the two knots at a ninety-degree angle to each other so that the dropper does not foul the leader back to the plug. Dropper leaders should be 8 to 12 inches long. A short dropper leader is usually better than a long one because it is less likely to foul.

I seldom use a wire leader when fishing with plugs. The plug is long enough to keep the fish's teeth away from the leader and a tough piece of monofilament leader will absorb the other abrasions. Wire leaders are used at times when big bluefish are actively feeding because other blues may try to take a plug out of the mouth of a hooked fish. This is not a common occurrence but it does happen and a short shot of wire, no more than 6 inches, will save your plug and your fish. I recommend braided wire of 60-pound-test connected to the snap and swivel with the proper-sized sleeves. You can purchase these leaders already made up by companies such as Berkley.

Metal Lures

The metal lure of choice not only for Atlantic Coast surf fishermen but for anglers all over the world is the Hopkins. This hammered stainless steel lure is almost indestructible and can be fished in a number of ways. The most common fishing method is to cast out and retrieve the lure much as you would do with a plug. The Hopkins has an easy swimming motion that works with a fairly slow retrieve. A fast retrieve will only make the lure swim faster. I don't think you can crank it in fast enough to spoil the action and make it twist. I have run the Hopkins over the surface as if it were a baitfish trying to escape, and even at this speed the lure worked beautifully.

At the other end of the speed spectrum, you can allow the lure to sink, and drag it very slowly back to the beach. This method works very well in areas where the game fish are feeding on sand eels. The Hopkins will stir up puffs of sand, just as an escaping sand eel might, and this will draw the attention of blues, weaks, and stripers. Big channel bass have also fallen victim to a slowly worked Hopkins lure.

The KastMaster is another excellent metal lure. It has an aerodynamic shape that allows it to cast like a bullet and it will not spin in the water to twist your line.

Both the KastMaster and the Hopkins lure will work well with a single hook replacing the treble. Some anglers think a single hook sets better than a treble and everyone agrees the single is easier to dislodge from a fish's mouth. In addition to the single hook you can add some bucktail hair or a rubber worm that will further enhance the lure's attractiveness.

Diamond jigs, such as those made by Bridgeport, can be used at times in the surf. The models that incorporate a tube lure over the hook have an excellent swimming action at a moderate-to-slow retrieve. Due to their heavy weight and smooth design diamond jigs cast very well and sink quickly. They can work well on windy days when the surf is rough and you want to get a lure out as far as possible and then have it stay close to the bottom.

There are many types of metal lures produced in various localities that have found favor with local anglers. You will find these in the tackle shops that cater to surf fishermen. Most are of good quality, but it is a good idea to inspect each product for proper construction, especially the hook used and its connection to the lure. Metal spoons do not work too well in the surf because they are light and have a good deal of wind resistance, which makes them difficult to cast. You can use a 1- to 3-ounce trolling sinker between the standing line and the leader to add some casting weight but this also dampens the action of the spoon and will make the rig less sensitive to a strike. It is a rare occurrence when fish won't hit any lure other than a spoon, but it does happen. The first run of bluefish through Indian River Inlet on the Delaware Coast each spring has a particular preference for Tony Acetta 141 spoons and you will need additional weight on the line if you want the lure to reach the fish.

Bucktails and Jigs

If given a choice of only one lure, I would always take a bucktail jig. It is the most versatile lure ever made and I do believe it will catch anything that swims. Unfortunately, surf fishing is not the best place for a bucktail. Once again, it is the casting ability of the lure, not its action, that prohibits its performance in the surf.

Bucktails can be deadly on some bottom feeders such as summer flounder. I use a double rig with the bucktails spaced 6 to 10 inches apart. One rig that works well is similar to the dropper setup. Instead of a plug at the end of the leader I use a 1-ounce bucktail and I replace the dropper fly with a half-ounce jig. You can also tie both bucktails directly to the leader using either a dropper loop, improved clinch knot, or palomar. I think the bucktails work better if they are separated from the line and have some freedom of movement.

The spotted or speckled sea trout is another species that is partial to the bucktail. It will hit these lures as well as plain jig heads decorated with a plastic worm or Twister Tail lure. The Scotchline Speck Rig is a very popular setup anywhere along the coast speckled trout are likely to show. It is a pre-tied double bucktail rig and comes in many different colors. The hair is not real bucktail but a nylon substance that seems to attract the trout just as well as the real thing.

Bucktail or jig fishing in the surf is seldom done with conventional

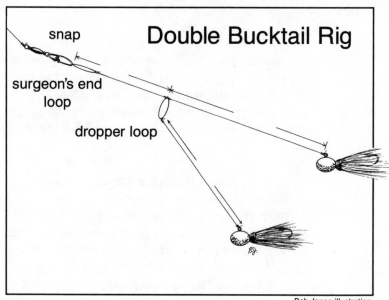

Double Bucktail Rig

snap

surgeon's end loop

dropper loop

Bob Jones illustration.

tackle. Due to the light weight and size of the bucktail, a one-handed spinning rod about 7 feet long and matched to a reel filled with 10- or 12-pound line works best. The light line will further improve your casting distance with the jig.

Both speckled trout and flounder tend to feed very close to the beach. This is another reason the bucktail can be used on them. If you had to cast 100 yards out to reach these fish you would have to find something other than a bucktail to use to catch them.

You can purchase large heavy bucktails but they don't work well on flounder and trout because these fish are feeding on small baits. The big bucktails would work with bluefish but the hair and paint on the lure is soon removed by the blue's teeth. Plugs or metal lures stand up better under this type of abuse.

A plain jig head can be decorated with any number of rubber lures that come in myriad sizes, shapes, and colors. Green Mr. Twister Curly Tail Grubs are very effective in the surf, especially for speckled trout. Flounder generally prefer white.

The folks at Uncle Josh's make several products that work very well in the surf. Their pork rind strips in white or green and the black eel do an excellent job when rigged on a jig head.

Don't overlook fresh bait as an addition to your bucktail jig. Strips of squid, shark belly, mullet, and whole sandworms will add action and scent to your lure. If fish are feeding close to the beach it may be easier to present the bait at the end of a jig rather than on a top-bottom or single-hook rig. The jig will work easily along the bottom and the lighter tackle will help you feel the hit from the smaller fish.

Tackle Transportation

There are some serious logistical problems facing the surf fisherman. The biggest problem is getting you and your tackle up to the surf with a minimum of effort. Those who own four-wheel-drive beach buggies won't have too much trouble, but those who must walk from the car to the beach should keep the size and the weight of their load as small as possible.

I don't know how fishermen survived before the invention of the plastic 5-gallon bucket, but now that we have this wonderful device, let's put it to good use. You should be able to get all the supplies you need for a day's surf fishing into one of these buckets, which you can carry in one hand. Rods, sand spikes, coolers, and other items that won't fit in the bucket will be carried in your other hand or strung over your shoulder.

If you try to carry everything you own up to the surf you will be too tired to fish when you get there. Keep your tackle selection down to a reasonable level and you won't have so many storage problems.

Two rods and reels will be more than one angler can handle. You will need two sand spikes to hold the rods and I have found that the white plastic variety sold at most seashore tackle shops do an admirable job. They are strong but light, and if you drill a hole at the tip of each one and run through it a piece of cord long enough to hold the sand spike over your shoulder you will be able to carry them with a minimum of effort.

You will need a half-dozen rigs, spare hooks, some 4- to 6-ounce sinkers, a fillet knife, a bait knife, waders or wading shoes, bait, cold drinks, and something to eat. If it looks like rain, take some rain gear. If it could get cold, take a jacket or sweater.

I do not take a big cooler along when I walk up on the beach. Generally, I don't plan to stay there all day, so I don't need the cooler for food and any fish I plan to keep can be buried in the sand, above the high-tide mark, until I head back. Bait and a few cold drinks will fit easily into a small lunch cooler. I do not suggest putting sandwiches and fresh bait into the same cooler. Not only will the smell of the bait penetrate the food, but you may also end up with food poisoning from the bacteria in the bait moving over to the sandwiches. Pack some peanut butter and jelly sandwiches and keep them in a separate plastic bag.

The smaller tackle boxes, such as the Plano Mini Magnum series or similar models made by Fenwick, are perfect for this type of fishing. They will hold your sinkers, some extra hooks, a few lures, terminal tackle, and other odds and ends while still fitting into your bucket.

Some anglers cut notches or holes along the rim of the bucket and hang their rigs and lures from these. This does keep the tackle from tangling, but I have caught myself and a very good pair of waders on these exposed hooks.

A new item on the market is the Fast Fete Bait Board, invented by a New Jersey fisherman. It is a plastic cover that fits perfectly over the top of any five-gallon bucket. There is a slot to keep your knife handy, and the smooth hard surface is perfect for cutting bait. It covers half of the opening and will shade the contents while still allowing air to flow and keep your bait or lunch from drying out.

One additional item that some may find necessary is a beach chair. I had a disk removed from my back a few years ago and now I cannot stand for long periods of time. I know I would catch more fish if I stood up and held the rod, but sand spikes and beach chairs are a more comfortable alternative.

Surf-Fishing Apparel

Surf fishermen along the East Coast are likely to encounter every type of weather condition, from arctic cold to tropic heat. Fish do not mind the weather conditions that keep most fishermen safe at home. You will have to dress properly or suffer the consequences of an un-relenting Mother Nature.

Chest waders are an absolute must for surf fishing. Hip boots will not work because, unlike a trout stream where boots are at home, the ocean has a nasty habit of sending waves onto your body that often break well above your waist. I have tried hip boots on several occasions and always ended up with wet legs and feet.

You must remember that the edge of the ocean is a very wet place. The breaking waves create a fine mist that will soon soak through ordinary clothing. In the summer this mist can be refreshing, but on a cold November night it can be bone chilling. The only protection against such a soaking is a good tough set of foul-weather gear. I have used Helly Hansons for many years and they have stood up to the worst abuse possible and are still as good as new. You must have very durable goods because your rain suit will always be in close contact with fish hooks, gaffs, knives, and myriad other sharp objects that can tear or puncture the most expensive foul-weather clothing on the market.

My Hellys are old and Gore-Tex was not available when I bought them. If it had been I probably would have purchased something with a Gore-Tex liner. This product has the unique ability to keep water out while letting moisture from your body pass through. I have a set of Remington Waterfowl hunting clothes with Gore-Tex, and they keep me warm and dry under weather conditions that are much worse than any I would encounter while fishing.

Waders must either be very tough or very inexpensive. Good-quality heavy waders are fine for cold-weather fishing, but I have used the Red Ball Adirondack waders for several years and have been pleased with their performance. These are good-quality waders but they are not as heavy as some of the more expensive models. This is more comfortable if you must wear the wader for long periods of time or if you have to do a lot of walking with them on.

The thinner waders do not protect you from cold water as well as the insulated models, but I have found a pair of heavy pants and insulated underwear will keep me warm when the water is cold. The uninsulated Helly Hanson rain gear should be worn over a wool sweater, heavy chamois shirt, and long underwear when used during periods of cold weather. Insulated rain gear will keep you warmer but can restrict your movement when casting or trying to fight a fish.

Wave action can cause some serious problems for anglers dressed against the cold. If you are knocked down into the surf by a wave, you can drown before you regain your footing. I suggest you keep your waders belted as tight as possible and don't venture far from shore. A few extra feet added to your casting distance is not worth your life.

Walking in the surf without some sort of protection for your feet is very foolish. You are likely to cut your foot on any number of objects in the wash or on the beach. A cut on your foot will quickly fill up with sand bringing on the chance of serious infection. Cleaning this sand out of an open wound is not an experience you will want to relive. Wear an old pair of canvas boat shoes when the weather is too warm for waders. They do feel a bit odd but you will soon become accustomed to this and the insurance against foot injury is well worth the discomfort.

Warm-weather fishing can be done in a pair of shorts or a swimming suit. If sea nettles are a problem you may want to wear a pair of long pants.

No matter what the weather, you should wear a hat. This not only protects those of us with thinning hair against sunburn, but it also shades the eyes and makes it easier to see what's going on in the surf.

A good pair of polarized sunglasses are as indispensable as the hat. Unless it is after dark I always wear my sunglasses, because even on an overcast day they help me see through the water and make it much easier to find color changes. They also reduce glare and save wear and tear on the eyes.

Protection from the sun is a very important consideration for everyone who spends time outside. The increasing incidence of skin cancer related to exposure to the sun's ultraviolet rays makes it wise to use a sun-blocking product at all times. I use a #15 blocking lotion on my body and a #22 blocker on my face and hands. Both of these products allow the skin to tan, but protect it from the rays that do damage. The Berkley Company currently produces a series of sun-blocking products that are not supposed to impart a bad scent to your bait or lures. These come in a variety of strengths, with the lower numbers containing less of the blocking agent.

When dressing for the surf, protection from the elements should be your first concern and comfort the second. Keep in mind that even the hottest day will be followed by a cool night on the beach. Summer can also produce heavy thunderstorms in the afternoon, so I suggest a rain jacket be part of your standard surf-fishing equipment.

There is a new product on the market that could be of use to the surf fisherman. These are neoprene waders and they are supposed to be light and warm. I have not tried a pair of these as yet, but several associates have used them and were pleased with the results. At the present time they are quite expensive, but the price could come down if more manufacturers enter this market.

CHAPTER 3

BAITS

The vast majority of fish caught in the surf, or anywhere else for that matter, are taken on some type of natural bait. Choosing exactly what type of bait to use and when to use it can be as difficult as selecting and presenting the proper artificial lure. To paraphrase Mr. Lincoln, "Some baits will fool some of the fish all of the time, some baits will fool all of the fish some of the time, but no bait will fool all of the fish all of the time." You have to pick the right bait and put it in the right place at the right time if you want to catch fish.

Bait should be selected with the same care you would use if you were going to eat it yourself. Look for good color, firm texture, and clean smell. If you are buying baitfish, check the eyes to make sure they are bright and clear.

Live baits should be alive. Look for any injury to the bait that could kill it before you get to the fishing grounds. Look carefully at the other baits in the tank to be sure all of them are in good condition. If many have already died, the others probably won't last very long.

As with any product, it is the dealer who has been in business for a long time, has a big inventory, and a background of satisfied customers, that will probably give you the highest quality product and the best service. Keeping bait fresh or alive is not an easy task and the dealer who has been doing the job successfully for a number of years has the experience required to deliver what you want. But remember—all of the bait dealer's hard work and your hard-earned money will be wasted if you do not keep the bait alive or fresh after you receive it.

Once again, you should treat your bait as if it were food. Keep all fresh baits in a cooler with generous amounts of ice. It is not a good idea to let the bait lie on the ice or sit in the melted water because this can cause it to become soft. Protect your baits by putting them in plastic bags and keeping them as dry as possible.

Live baits require a considerable amount of work and equipment to keep them healthy and happy. Crabs and worms will keep in a cool dry place, but fish and eels must have well-aerated water to stay alive. Sand crabs, peeler crabs, calico crabs, green crabs, fiddler crabs, and almost any other crab you can name will catch a variety of fish, but you must keep them alive until you are ready to put them on the hook. A cooler half-full of ice with a board or plastic covering separating the ice from the crabs is the best way to keep them alive. Dead crabs deteriorate quickly and are not much good for anything except chum. Do not put the crabs in an airtight container or they will suffocate from lack of oxygen.

Keeping baitfish alive is quite a chore but it can be done. You will need a large container capable of holding 15 to 20 gallons of water if you plan to keep three or four dozen spot- or mullet-size baits alive for ten to twelve hours. Bigger baits such as mackerel or herring require considerably more water and the container should be round-shaped so that they won't bunch up in a corner and die.

My bait tank is a converted 86-quart Igloo cooler. I use a 350-gallon-per-hour bilge pump to circulate the water through a piece of PVC pipe with holes in it to let the water flow out. The pipe is capped at one end and attached to the bilge pump through a hose at the other end. The leads from the pump should be connected directly to the battery with alligator clips so that they can be easily removed when you aren't using the tank.

It should be apparent that this type of live-bait tank is not for the walk-on surf fisherman. You need a four-wheel-drive vehicle to carry it about. Those who do not have such a convenience may use a 5-gallon bucket with a portable aerator to keep up to a dozen small baits alive. This bucket full of water and bait will still weigh you down but it is certainly more manageable than an 86-quart cooler.

Eels fall into a category all their own. You can keep them alive in wet seaweed, but they do have a nasty habit of not staying where they belong. I use ice water to keep them dormant until I need them. A 48-quart cooler with a gallon or two of water mixed with a gallon or two of crushed ice will keep the eels alive as well as in their place.

A good friend of mine was fishing the Nantucket beach with another man in the other fellow's new Chevy Blazer. They had two dozen eels in the back of the Blazer as they set out on the long drive over a very rough road to the selected fishing spot. When they arrived, they discovered that all of the eels had taken leave of the box and were crawling all over the back of the vehicle. My friend reached in, selected a good-looking specimen, baited up, and left the owner of the Blazer to find the rest of the eels. He found twenty-three of them that night and one more several warm days later. That wonderful new-car smell had been replaced by the very distinct odor of something dead, which still lingered when the Blazer was finally sold.

You can purchase several varieties of live-bait tanks, but most of these are more suited to use on a boat than on the beach. Most have a rounded shape, which is great for bunker and herring but can be difficult to mount in your vehicle.

Regardless of where you fish or with what types of bait, you must keep it as fresh as possible. Frozen bait will work but it is a poor substitute for fresh. (The exception to this is frozen squid, which works well thawed as bait.) Most frozen bait will turn to mush as soon as it thaws out. Some of this can be prevented if you use a large quantity of kosher salt on the bait before it enters the freezer. Few if any commercial bait dealers go to this trouble and expense, so their baits will turn soft when defrosted.

If I had to buy bait in a strange area I would always choose the freshest bait available and try to avoid frozen. If a bait is fresh, it was probably caught locally within a day or two before you bought it. This means that type of bait is currently available in local waters and is what the fish probably are feeding on. This same process will work in any location, even the area you fish every weekend.

Gathering your own bait will insure its freshness, but it can be hard work. Most of the bait I use is purchased from a local shop because it is easy and not expensive when compared to the other costs involved with surf fishing. I don't believe I have ever spent more than ten or fifteen dollars for a day's supply of bait, but I have spent much more than that for a day's supply of fuel to run my vehicle down to the shore.

Those who insist on doing it themselves will need some equipment to gather their bait. Crabs can be potted in standard crab traps. Be sure you are in compliance with local state laws before you set your traps.

You must cull your catch to return any illegal-sized crabs or those carrying egg sacks. Some species of crabs are not protected by laws while others, especially blue crabs, come under very rigid regulations.

Fiddler crabs can be collected from mud flats at low tide. Green crabs are usually potted over the same type of mud bottom at high tide. Mole crabs, or sandfleas, can be captured along the surf line by digging them out of the sand. A special device, known as a sandflea rake, will make this job much quicker and easier.

Mud flats will also produce various types of sea worms, depending on which part of the East Coast they call home. Bloodworms are found in New England, sandworms in the middle Atlantic region, and red worms along the southern coast. The bloodworms and sandworms work well in the surf, but I have found the red worms are too small and brittle for use off the beach.

Various types of mussels and clams can be found all along the beach and in the nearby tidal marshes. Many species of fish, from channel bass to croaker, can be caught on clams and mussels, but for some reason they are not a favorite bait among most surf fishermen.

Catching your own baitfish can pose quite a challenge. A cast-net will bring in surface-swimming bait such as mullet, while a haul-seine is best for spot or silversides. A cast-net will take spot in shallow water and you will see them used with great success in the fall all along the surf line.

Throwing a cast-net requires some amount of skill, which is best learned through practice. The idea is to toss the net out so that it spreads open into a big circle before it hits the water. I hold the lead line in my right hand while my left hand holds the rest of the net. To toss it, I turn my body to the left, away from the water, and then spin around back to my right as I throw the net toward the target.

Remember to secure the line from the net to your wrist before you throw the rig. I watched an experienced fisherman toss a very expensive net into a very deep tidal creek because he forgot to take this precaution. It took quite a few casts with a grappling hook to retrieve the net, and by then the bait was gone.

Working a haul-seine is a two-man operation. It is best done over a hard sand bottom during high tides after dark. This usually requires a loss of sleep and at least one of the operators will step in a hole and fill his waders with water.

One bait catcher works his end of the net close to the beach, while the other, who drew the short straw, works as far out as his net will reach or until the water becomes too deep for safe operation. The net is dragged for several hundred yards or until one of the operators hollers "Uncle." Then the man on the deep end works back toward the beach, keeping the net's lead line on the bottom at all times.

A belly will form in the net as you drag it up on the beach. This will contain whatever you have managed to catch and may include anything from the bait you were after to sea nettles and crabs. These and other little stinging and pinching creatures can make culling the catch quite an adventure, especially at night.

Some types of bait are used only in specific locations, while others are used all along the East Coast. Each is fished in a specific manner and it pays to know how to prepare the various types you may encounter.

Squid

I suspect that every tackle shop along the coast has a supply of squid. It is a universal bait that can be used in a variety of applications.

Unless the squid is very small you will use it in pieces. The size and shape of the piece is determined by the type of fish you are trying to catch or the type of bait you are trying to imitate.

The first step when preparing a squid is to remove the pink outer skin to reveal the white meat underneath. If the meat is not pure white the squid may not be fresh and it probably will not work as bait.

Frozen squid must be thawed quickly and is easier to work with if you clean it while it is still partially frozen. Squid that has thawed out completely over a long period of time will often have discolored meat, and for some reason this pink meat will not appeal to game fish.

After the squid is skinned you should cut off the head and then split open the body. Save the tentacles; they make great baits for small fish such as spot and croaker. There is usually a large deposit of black ink inside the squid. This must be washed out and the insides, including that little piece of plastic packed in every squid, must be discarded.

The remainder will be a flat piece of white squid that can be cut to suit your purpose. I use long, thin strips for flounder and weakfish because they like a little action in their bait. Fish with small mouths, like northern kingfish, require a small piece of bait on a small hook.

Because squid is so tough it makes a wonderful addition to lures such as bucktails and jigs. My all-time favorite flounder rig is a white bucktail with a 3- or 4-inch piece of squid on the hook.

It is a good idea to cut up all the squid you expect to use in one day before you begin to fish. This not only keeps you prepared for action, but also keeps the rest of the squid from thawing out and turning pink.

Put the cut-up squid in a Tupperware or Rubbermaid container, seal it tight, and keep it on ice. Do not allow your bait to come into contact with fresh water because this will turn it into mush.

Just because squid is available during the entire season does not mean it is the best bait to use all year. I find it works well on flounder, spot, croaker, and sometimes it works on sea trout. Bluefish will eat anything, but most of the time they like fresh fish and not squid. Summer is usually the best time to use a squid bait because this is when the smaller fish are around.

Worms

At some time in their life cycles most saltwater fish feed on some type of worm. Species such as northern kingfish and spot will continue to eat this type of bait while others, such as weakfish, add more variety to their diet. This early attraction to worms stays with these fish and a worm bait will draw strikes from some species not normally associated with this type of bait.

I have caught summer flounder and weakfish on bloodworms while fishing for other species. The mighty striped bass will take a bloodworm or sandworm with as much gusto as he will a plug or live bait. The bottom line is that worms work, and they work on a variety of fishes throughout the season.

There are two ways to rig a worm bait. One keeps the bait short by threading it on a long-shanked hook, such as the Chestertown. The other method allows the worm to stream out by threading only the head on the hook.

The short version is required if you plan to catch such fish as northern kingfish, spot, or croaker. These fish are nibblers and they will eat off any bait not directly on the hook. They are light strikers and you need to get the hook and the bait into their mouths so that they will hook themselves.

A long flowing worm bait works well for weakfish, flounder, and

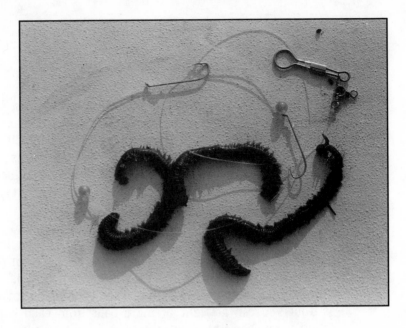

Bloodworm baits work best with long, thin Chestertown hooks and without a float.

striped bass. These species have large mouths and will easily take the entire worm with one gulp. They also have a tendency to hit the head of a bait, so having the barb of the hook in this location is a good idea. I like a wide-gap English-style hook when worm fishing for weaks, flounder, or bass.

The two most common worms used as bait by surf fishermen are bloodworms and sandworms. Bloods are usually more expensive, costing up to six dollars a dozen but they are tougher and stay on the hook a little longer. Bloodworms have a longer shelf life than do sandworms, so you will find them sold in shops that are a long way from their native New England coast.

Sandworms are even uglier than bloodworms. They are a sick-looking blue-to-red color and lots of little leg-like protrusions stick out of their sides from head to tail. Generally, a sandworm is longer than a bloodworm and sandworms usually cost less per dozen, so you get more baits for your buck.

I have used both of these worms and I haven't found any fish that preferred one over the other. If you can find sandworms where you fish, use them. If not, you will have to go with the more expensive bloodworms.

Crabs

Any crab you are likely to find along the East Coast can be used for bait. The spider and the horseshoe crab are the only exceptions to this rule because they don't have enough meat in their shells to make a bait.

Peeler or shedder crabs are the premolting stages of hard-shelled crabs such as blue, calico, and speckled. The most available of these is the blue crab, which can be used on almost every type of fish that swims along the coast.

Unlike a hard crab that you can simply cut up and use, the peeler must first be peeled. Start by removing the apron, then peel off the hard back-shell. Under this you will find a soft shell that for some reason is almost irresistible to fish. Cut the peeler into sections, using the segments on the underside as a guide. When fishing for small species such as trout you can get four or more baits from each half of the crab. Channel bass like a big meal, so give them at least a quarter of the crab.

Crabs do not lend themselves to surf casting because they are difficult to keep on the hook. I find the best method is to run the point of the hook through a leg hole and not through the shell. Once in the leg hole, the hook will not come out as easily as it does when placed through the shell; the hook tends to crack the shell and then it has nothing to hold on to.

Casting a crab bait calls for a bit of finesse. Don't try to launch the bait into orbit. Use a smooth cast so that you won't whip the bait off the hook. Remember, a 300-foot cast with bait still on the hook will catch more fish than will a 600-yard cast with no bait.

Crabs can often be a bait of opportunity. If you are using some other type of bait and it is either being eaten or mauled by unseen creatures, you are probably fishing in a hotbed of crab activity. Eventually you will catch one of these bait stealers, and instead of stomping it into a mangled mess, try cutting it up and using it for bait. Be assured that if there are that many crabs out there, sooner or later something will show up to eat them.

Sandfleas, or mole crabs, are usually caught in the surf and used immediately. I try to encourage my kids to dig some up so that I can use them for bait, but this ploy is not always successful and I end up digging my own. These are excellent baits for pompano, king whiting, and spot. All of these fish feed close to the beach, where the sandfleas are found in abundance.

Sandfleas, or mole crabs, make good baits for a variety of bottom fish.

Hooking a mole crab is easy. Just bring the point in from the underside and out through the top of the shell. Try to put it on as close to the middle as possible. Once again, a soft cast is required to keep this bait on the hook.

Many anglers will use dental floss, elastic string, or some other material to tie their crab on the hook. I find this a sloppy, time-consuming process that usually is not necessary. A little care in putting the crab on the hook and a gentle cast will deliver your crab bait to the fish.

Clams and Mussels

Black drum is one species that has a particular craving for a big gooey clam bait. Striped bass and channel bass will also take this bait because it is part of their natural diets.

Mussels are used for most of the smaller species, but weakfish also find them quite appealing. If you surf-fish over rocks or near a wreck, your mussel bait could put a tautog on your hook.

Big sea clams are available in some bait stores, but may be hard to find because they are not traditional baits in every location. Hard-shell clams are usually found at the seafood market and they can be a bit expensive. You will find the larger, or chowder, clams cost less per pound than do cherrystone clams. This works to the fisherman's advantage because he wants the bigger, tougher clams that stay on the hook much better than do the small but tasty cherrystones.

Mussels have recently become available in almost every seafood store but they are much too expensive to buy as bait. Fortunately, they abound on almost every rock, piling, sod bank, and other structure that is exposed at low tide. It is easy to gather enough for a day's fishing in a few minutes of picking. I suggest a pair of cotton gloves to protect your hands against sharp shells and other hazards.

Clams and mussels are soft baits but each has a tough foot that will hold your hook. The bigger the clam, the bigger and tougher the foot. If you must cut up your clam, be sure to cut it across the foot and not down the side. You want pieces of the foot for bait, not the soft stomach, which will quickly fall off the hook. Clams work well on big hooks, but mussels are best saved for small fish and smaller hooks. Once again, a soft, low cast will insure delivery of the bait to the fish.

Shrimp

When shrimp sold for a dollar-fifty a pound it was a very popular bait. Today this same product goes for five to six dollars a pound and its popularity as a bait has fallen off considerably.

Used primarily for small fish, a shrimp is usually cut into three or four pieces before being put on the hook. A live shrimp under a popper is very popular with folks who wade the southern surf for speckled trout. Cut shrimp works well for specks and gray trout plus most of the small bottom fish. Whole fresh shrimp can be used for channel bass and large-size trout.

Due to the high cost, many tackle shops no longer stock fresh shrimp. If you can't find it at the bait store you will have to try the local seafood store and pay the premium price.

Fresh Fish

There are many species of baitfish available along the East Coast. The more common include mullet, bunker, herring, and mackerel. No matter the species, the bait is used in the same manner. Small fish can be rigged whole, while larger specimens should be cut into pieces. The

Insert the shank of the hook into the vent and bring it out of the mouth.

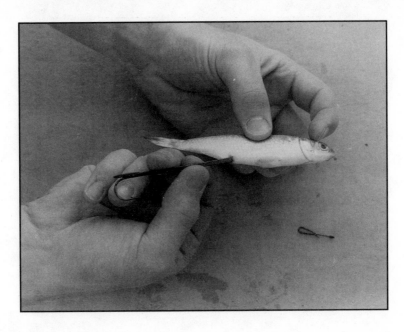

final size of the bait should approximate what is available in the waters you plan to fish. It should also be tailored to the size of the fish you expect to catch. Keep in mind that big fish eat small baits and small fish only steal big baits.

Finger mullet, spot, and bunker can be used either whole or cut up. When I rig them whole I like to use a Mustad Ryder hook because it holds the bait in a natural-looking manner.

Large mackerel, herring, and mullet will be cut into chunks or fillets and used on larger hooks. You should cut the pieces large enough so that the hook can pass through the bait twice. This helps hold it on during the cast and keeps it on in the surf should a fish strike but fail to get hooked.

Filleted strips of bait will move about in the current, adding a bit of action to the bait. These strips are also softer than a similar piece of bait with the bone left in, so they may come off the hook or you may find all the meat eaten and only the skin left.

Use a fillet knife to fillet your bait and a boning knife to cut it into pieces. A fillet knife is not made to cut through bone and it could slip and cut *you*.

There is no reason not to use every part of your baitfish. Predators are not picky eaters: they take the head, tail, and the middle of the fish,

BAITS

The line clip goes
through the eye of
the hook.

Determine where
the point of the
Mustad Ryder hook
should go.

SURF FISHING THE ATLANTIC COAST

Insert the large barb in the tail of the mullet.

Insert the small hook behind the head of the bait.

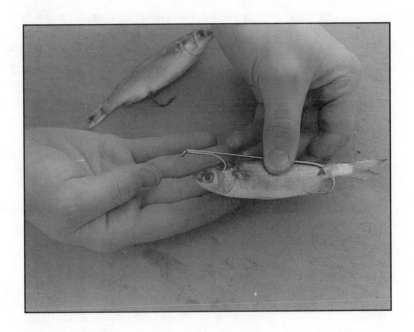

Mullet cut into bite-sized pieces that will go on the two-hook rig.

so why should you throw anything away? I have followed people on the beach who left little piles of mullet heads and tails after fishing for an hour or two. This made the sea gull population very happy, as well as the guy who sells them their bait, but I feel it is wasteful fishing. The head and tail sections are the toughest parts of a baitfish. These pieces stay on the hook and they don't fall apart as quickly in the water as do the softer middle sections.

Scaling a bait before you cut it up can be a good idea for such species as mullet. These fish have big scales that can impede or divert the point of your hook as you try to thread it through a bait. I have had the hook diverted by a scale to a point dangerously close to my thumb. Removal of the scales before cleaning will solve this problem.

Live Baits

After catching or buying a live bait, it seems foolish to me when an angler will hook it so that the fish is probably dead before it hits the

A wide-gap hook and a small float works well with cut bait.

Bring the hook completely through the bait.

A spot rigged on a Mustad Ryder hook, with wire leader and float.

water. The object of obtaining live bait is to fish with it while it is still alive. Just getting the bait out of the live well can injure it. Use a small dip net, available in many tackle shops and in all tropical fish stores, to lift your bait out of the tank. This not only protects the fish but also keeps your hand out of the cold water.

There are many theories about the best place to hook a live bait. Many anglers place the hook just under the back bone, ahead of the dorsal fin. Others put it close to the base of the tail. I have found drawbacks to both of these placements. When the fish is hooked close to the backbone you run a risk of serious injury, which will soon kill your bait. The backbone is as important to the life of a fish as it is to the life of any other vertebrate, so I try to keep the hook as far from it as possible.

Most baitfish have very hard ridges across the top of their heads, between their eyes. If you carefully run the hook into one eye socket, under this hard ridge, and then out of the opposite eye socket, you won't injure the bait and it will live for a long time on your hook. Do not run the hook through the fish's eye but through the socket at the corner of the eye. When it is hooked in this manner, it is almost impossible to snap the bait off the hook during a cast. When you retrieve bait back to the beach the fish will be moving in a normal

SURF FISHING THE ATLANTIC COAST

manner, head first, not sideways or backwards as it would if hooked in the back or tail.

I have used this method with live spot, mullet, and mackerel, and it worked perfectly. Live herring and bunker are not quite as hardy as the other baits, so hooking them in this manner should help keep them alive.

CHAPTER 4

CASTING

Accurate casting is essential to successful surf fishing. You cannot catch fish if your bait or lure remains on the beach, and it is difficult to catch them if your casts are inconsistent or inaccurate. The only method for developing a successful casting technique is practice, but before you begin there are a few facts you should know.

The beginning surf caster should concentrate on style—not on distance. You will never achieve the latter until you master the former. In all previous discussions on tackle, we stressed balanced gear that matched the size of the fisherman. It is impossible to cast effectively with unbalanced, unmatched tackle. The rod, reel, line, and weight must work in harmony with the caster or all of your physical effort will be wasted.

Physical size does carry some advantage, but smaller people can do almost as well if their tackle is matched to their requirements. Sue Ellingsworth is a little over five feet tall but she can consistently cast over 500 feet of line using a graphite rod and a matching reel built to her specifications. I am six-four and weigh 200 pounds. On a good day with a strong tail wind I can top 400 feet. Granted, Sue puts more time into her casting because she competes in tournaments, but her success proves that you can get your rig out to the fish no matter how big or small you may be.

The best place to begin surf casting is on the beach. You can practice on football fields or other large open areas, but the sinker is forever getting caught up on the grass and there are always other people around who may take exception to 4 or 5 ounces of lead flying in their direction.

The first thing to try for is accuracy. It is very important to have your cast going straight out from where you are standing into the water. If you are constantly casting to your left or right you will lose distance and foul the lines of those anglers fishing next to you. We all make misguided casts, and these can be forgiven, but the angler who is always tangled up with those who fish around him will soon wear out his welcome.

Start your casting off with a lob. This is quite easy, and although it won't get you much distance, it will keep you straight. Drop the weight 2 or 3 feet from the tip of the rod. Hold the rod directly over the top of your head with the reel just behind your back and the rod butt in front of your eyes. Pull down on the butt while you push out with the reel and the tip will move forward, bringing the weight along. When you feel maximum pressure on the line, release it and the weight will carry on out to sea.

This feeling for the correct time to release the line is the most difficult part of surf casting. You are trying to find the exact time when the rod is fully loaded and can transfer all of your energy into the weight. Rods, reels, and lines do not generate energy; they can only transmit it from you to the weight. The weight will pull the line from the reel.

Spinning reels have fixed spools, so once the weight is released it must overcome the resistance of the line to leave its resting place. Conventional reels have revolving spools, and this will actually throw the line off, reducing the drag felt by the weight and resulting in a longer cast. The key is keeping the spool revolving at the exact speed of the sinker as it sails out toward the horizon. If the spool is moving too slowly your distance will suffer. If it moves too fast you will be rewarded with a backlash. A little backlash is not bad because it means the line was moving off the reel fast enough to keep the drag at a minimum. A big backlash will test your patience as you try to untangle what appears to be a hopeless mess.

Digging out a backlash is not as hard as it looks. I have cleared some that demonstrated why the term "bird's nest" is often used to describe this phenomenon. Do not try to remove your backlash by pulling on the line. This will only compound matters because you will embed the line under itself and make it much harder to dig out.

A backlash is an overrun. The reel spool was spinning so fast that the line came off and then started to wind itself back on in the opposite direction. This creates loops that catch the line trying to come off the spool, stopping that procedure quite abruptly. If the sinker is still moving at top speed you will hear a very loud noise, not unlike a rifle shot, and watch as your rig sails on toward Africa completely unencumbered by any fishing line.

To dig the mess out of your reel you must find the loops and back the line away from them. Begin by slowly pulling line from your reel until you feel resistance. Look on the spool and you will see the cause of this resistance is a loop, under which the line has passed. Take one side of the loop and pull it as the spool now turns in the opposite direction. As you pull the loop out, the line will free up and you can begin to pull it again until the next loop is encountered.

The only backlashes I have seen that were beyond repair were made by tournament casters who made a slight miscalculation. Their sinkers travel so fast that the line ends up buried under many very tight loops that defy repair. The only solution is to cut it all off and respool.

Beginners will probably be happier with a spinning reel. The timing and coordination required to cast is difficult enough to master without the hassle of a backlashed reel.

The correct timing for releasing the line can be judged by where your sinker lands. If it lands behind your back, you didn't hold on long enough. If it lands at your feet, you probably held the line a bit too long. If the sinker lands on your head, you're getting closer.

The line should be held on the tip of your index finger. Release the line by straightening out your finger as the pressure of the line reaches maximum.

The drag on your reel must be tight enough to keep the line from slipping off as you load the rod. This line slippage will take some of the energy out of your cast and can take some of the skin off your finger. I normally work with a tight drag to control the fish when it is hooked, but you may wish to loosen the drag after each cast. Just don't forget to tighten it before you cast again.

Your thumb is used to control the line on a conventional reel. You hold it on the spool until you are ready to release the line, then use it to adjust the speed of the spool as the line plays out.

When I began my surf-fishing career the only conventional reels found on the beach were made by Penn or Ocean City. My choice was

The line should rest on your fingertip.

the Penn Squider with a heavy metal spool that required an educated thumb to control. Today I use a Penn 980 with counterbalance weights and magnetic controls. I still use my thumb, but the required expertise is not as critical as it once was.

The lob cast is a good way to begin, but once you get your timing lined up you will find this method is a bit restrictive. You can't get sufficient energy into the rod for any long-distance casting, and if the wind is blowing from any direction except directly behind you the line will belly out and further reduce your distance.

Distance is a relative term in surf casting. Tournament casters can top 700 feet, but they are using specialized tackle and a single sinker tied directly to their lines. In actual fishing conditions, where you must deliver not only the sinker but a rig, hook, leader, and bait, the distance of your cast will be cut down considerably.

There will be many fishing situations when accuracy will be much more important than distance. If there is a small sandbar or hole 50 yards off the beach, you will have to get your bait right there—not another 50 yards past the target or off to one side. Often, the fish will be feeding right in the white water inside the breakers. In this situation you must get your bait right in behind a breaking wave, so timing and accuracy will be important.

Distance casting can produce when the fish are far offshore. Big bluefish are notorious for feeding about one-and-a-half casts from the beach. False albacore also like to stay just out of range and they move up and down the beach very quickly, so you must put the line just ahead of them when they are 75 to 100 yards away.

The most effective cast I have found for getting a baited rig out a reasonable distance is something I would describe as a wind-up. Begin with 4 to 5 feet of line between the rod tip and the rig. Stand facing the water, then turn to your right or left and flip the sinker out behind you. In this position, if you are right-handed, you are facing down the beach to your right and the rod tip is pointed away from you at a slight angle in the opposite direction. The sinker should be on the sand and you will move the rod tip until the line comes tight.

The cast begins when you push away with your right hand while pulling back the butt with your left. The motion of your right hand is not unlike pitching a softball. As your arms push and pull on the rod, your body will pivot toward the water. It is the pivot motion that creates much of the energy that is transferred from you through the rod and into the sinker.

You should release the line and end the casting motion with the rod tip pointed at a ninety-degree angle to the surf. If it is pointed to the left or to the right, that is where your rig will end up. Casting is just like shooting: the projectile goes exactly where the shooter or caster aims. This may not be where he wanted it to go, but it *will* be where he pointed the rod or gun.

A variation of this method that can be used when standing in the water is to hold the sinker about 2 feet off the rod tip, keeping it just above the water's surface. The rod is still pointed down the beach to your left as you turn your body to the right at the start of the cast. You may have to hold the rod higher to keep the sinker or lure out of the surf.

I have seen many surf fishers try to snap their casts. This usually results in snapping off the rig. A smooth follow-through movement will produce the best results.

Casting soft baits such as peeler crabs, clams, or sandfleas requires a gentle touch. The wind-up method will work, but use a slightly slower turning motion and don't load the rod to its maximum potential.

Recently there has been a great deal of interest in the European style of long-distance surf casting. Many European beaches slope very gently and you must cast a long distance to reach the deep water where fish are found. In order to accomplish this, European surf fishers have developed a casting method that will deliver a 5-ounce sinker out to ranges of 700 feet and more on a consistent basis.

This system includes not only the casting method but the rods, reels, line, sinkers, rigs, and knots to make it work. The tackle employed by East Coast surf fishers will not propel anything out to those distances, and the tackle used by Europeans would be destroyed by a 20-pound bluefish.

American surf fishermen are developing rods, rigs, and terminal tackle that will cast long distances and land big fish. Right now, you can buy such tackle only from custom builders, but it should soon be available in surfside tackle shops.

John Holden of England was the man who made the European casting method popular in the United States. Using his own tackle, he cast 700 feet or more and made it look very easy. I watched him perform during a local contest at Cape Henlopen, Delaware, where the maximum distance marked on the field was 700 feet. Mr. Holden placed his sinker so far beyond the mark that it landed in some trees and he had to walk out to retrieve his weight. During this cast he delivered a running commentary on his technique. At this writing most American casters are still a long way from perfecting the European long-distance method.

The pendulum, or European, casting technique is not unlike the wind-up method most of us use in America. The difference is in the loading of the rod by swinging the sinker back over one's head and completely around to the left side. This motion is similar to a pendulum on a clock as it swings to its maximum apex in one direction before swinging back the other way. When you are casting, the rod is attached to the weight so that it extends to its maximum from the forces generated by the sinker. As the body unwinds with the cast, this energy is added to the rod and transferred to the sinker, greatly increasing the power used to propel it outward. The secret of the pendulum cast is in feeling exactly when the sinker has hit the top of its swing. Once again, practice is the key to success.

There are some peculiarities to the pendulum cast. If the sinker breaks off, it is likely to travel down the beach, not out to sea. This can make folks standing on your right a bit nervous as 4 or 5 ounces of lead whisk by their ears.

The pendulum cast will not work with two heavy weights. Trying to cast a 6-ounce sinker as well as a big chunk of cut bait will result in two pendulums swinging from the end of your rod, and neither one will be able to take advantage of the action.

The British normally do not fish with big baits. They use small hooks on short leaders that are clipped to the rig and do not move about during the cast. When the rig hits bottom the hooks are released to move about on the leaders.

Long casting rods are not suitable to Atlantic Coast fishing because they have a very fast tip for maximum casting power, and these same tips will collapse under the pressure of a big fish. The rods and rigs would work very well if you were trying to reach a school of croaker feeding inside a distant bar but would be out of place in the middle of a chopper bluefish blitz. Some surf fishers in the mid-Atlantic region have made their own rods that combine the power required for a pendulum cast with the strength needed to land a big fish.

The pendulum-style cast will improve distance when you are tossing artificials, especially metal lures. They are single projectiles with a leader the only additional tackle. I use a modified version of this cast when using these lures by swinging the weight behind my back before twisting around to cast. It doesn't load the rod as completely as a full pendulum cast but it is easier on my finger and gets the job done.

Most surf casters will use some type of protection on their casting finger if they fish with spinning tackle. The constant rubbing of the line over your fingertip during each cast can make that area very tender. A piece of white adhesive bandage works very well or you can purchase leather finger guards made especially for casting. The pendulum cast should never be attempted without protection for your finger.

Conventional-reel users may have a similar device for their thumbs. I have never been happy with any thumb guard I have tried so I keep on getting blisters. The first cast of the day is the worst to control because the line is still dry and easily builds up heat. Make this one a bit on the light side and wait until the line gets wet before you lean into it.

Should you desire to enter the long-casting tournament circuit or just want more information on the English pendulum cast, I suggest you pick up a copy of John Holden's books *Long Distance Casting* and *The Beach Fisherman's Tackle Guide*. Both are published by The Crowood Press in England, but they can be purchased at select tackle shops, book stores, or mail-order companies. *Salt Water Sportsman* magazine lists them in its library.

CHAPTER 5

WHERE TO FISH

Fishing the surf requires a knowledge of tides, currents, moon phases, water temperatures, and bottom structure. You must understand how fish find their food and how all of the above factors affect fish behavior. You don't have to be a fisheries biologist or an oceanographer, but unless you develop a feel for the fish's environment you will never become a proficient fisherman.

The ocean is a constantly moving body of water. It moves up and down with the tide and in and out with the current while the waves constantly break on the shore. Fish in the ocean must adapt to this movement; they cannot fight it or leave it, so they have evolved into creatures who use the moving water to locate food.

There are two factors that control the water in the ocean: the sun and moon, and wind. The tides are controlled by the moon and, to a lesser extent, by the sun. Waves are formed by the wind, and wind is created by differences in barometric pressures. These factors can create an infinite variety of sea conditions, some of which improve fishing success, and others of which keep you at home beside a warm fire.

Along the Atlantic Coast we have two tidal cycles each day. These are called *semidiurnal tides,* and are calculated by the federal government and published in *Tide Table for the East Coast of North and South America Including Greenland.* This book comes out annually and can be a help to those who travel to various surf-fishing areas. If you fish one area exclusively you can probably get a tide chart from a local tackle shop with information pertaining to this particular location.

You must know when tides will be high or low because there are some beaches that produce on different stages of the tide. A gradually sloping beach is normally devoid of fish on low water but may attract some attention on the flood. A sand spit may be exposed at low water so you can venture out and cast to fish holding offshore.

Low tide is the best time to check out a new piece of beach or your old favorite after a storm. When the tide is out you will be able to see most of the bars, sloughs, holes, and other structure that fish may frequent, make notes, and, as the tide comes back in, you will be able to fish those now-hidden features.

Current flow and direction are a direct result of tidal action. As the tide ebbs and floods it fills or empties bays, creeks, and rivers, as well as cuts, sloughs, holes, and wash-outs. As the water moves in and out of these impoundments, a current is created. How strong it will be and in which direction it will flow depends on the size of the body in question and its relationship to the beach.

A large body of water that must fill and empty through a small inlet will create strong currents around this opening. Places like Oregon Inlet, North Carolina; Indian River Inlet, Delaware; and Barnegat Inlet, New Jersey, are perfect examples of this type of current.

The current created at the mouth of a large body of water that empties directly into the ocean is considerable, but still not as fast as the current at a small inlet. The beaches where bays empty out are usually known as *points*. The Point at Cape Henlopen, Delaware, is an example of this. Sandy Point in New Jersey is where the Hudson River and Raritan Bay meet the Atlantic. These and similar locations have been surf-fishing hot spots since they were first discovered.

The most famous point along the East Coast is Cape Point on Hatteras Island in North Carolina. No bay or river empties out here, but the Gulf Stream and the Labrador Current collide over Diamond Shoals, creating this finger of sand. Both of these currents are like rivers within the sea and should not be confused with the common tidal currents found along most beaches.

The direction of the current is important because fish receive all of their information from the water and, just as a deer will stand with his nose into the wind, so a fish will swim into the current. The more water that passes through his nose and mouth, the easier it is for him to detect the presence of nearby food.

Current can also work against a fish. These animals must conserve their energy because if they use more energy to catch food than that food can replace they will starve to death. Unlike most humans, who eat more than they can use, fish must feed in the most efficient manner possible. This is why you seldom find fish in the middle of an inlet when the current is running full bore. They are more likely to be closer to shore, behind a rock or bridge piling, where they can benefit from the rushing water without having to fight against the current.

Along every beach I have fished, the prevailing currents move up and down or from left to right. These currents can be so strong at times that you cannot hold bottom with a reasonably sized sinker. Any time you need more than 6 ounces to keep your bait in one place, the current is really ripping. I have seen times when 8 ounces or more were swept back to the beach in a matter of minutes.

The intensity of the current is controlled by the phase of the moon. If it is a full or new moon the tidal flow will be greater and this will result in a stronger current flow. Storms, especially northeasters, also make the current run heavier. These blows usually uproot lots of sea-weed and the accompanying higher-than-normal tides flood marshes, carrying off tons of dead grass. All of this mess ends up in the surf, where it combines with the strong current to make fishing virtually impossible.

Currents and tides do not keep the same schedule. Generally, the current will change direction an hour or two after the flood or ebb tide. The U.S. government publishes a book that gives you these times for the East Coast. *Tidal Current Tables for the Atlantic Coast of North America* will list many points along the coast, but it may not have the exact spot where you plan to fish. To figure the tidal and current changes for places not listed in *Tidal Current Tables,* you will have to guesstimate from personal observation.

As an example, say your favorite fishing hole lies 10 miles north of a point listed in the Tide Tables. You have fished there a few times and it seems like the tide and current change about an hour later than the times they are listed in the Tide and Current Tables. This would be normal because tidal change occurs later as you move north. With this observation and a little figuring, you will be able to arrive at the proper stage of the tide when fishing should be at its best.

The wind can affect the height of the tide but it does not affect the time of high or low tide. Only the moon and sun control the time of the tides and, so long as they don't fall out of the sky, you can set your clock by their progress.

Wind direction and intensity can bring fish to the beach or keep them away. A southwest wind in the spring or fall will put red drum on the Point at Cape Hatteras. A moderate east wind will bring big bluefish to the Pocket at Indian River Inlet in Delaware during the fall. A strong northeast wind will curtail all fishing activity along much of the East Coast. A northwest wind will calm the sea and clear the surf. You must observe the effects of winds on your particular fishing area. The more time you spend fishing and exploring, the more likely you will be to find a lee shore in almost any wind condition.

The time of day when you plan to fish can be a deciding factor in your success. A perfect tide with the right wind and current is not likely to be as productive at noon as it would be at dusk or dawn. Fish are sensitive about moving into shallow water when the sun is high because they feel more vulnerable to predators. Don't think you can't catch fish during the day—you can—but your chances are improved if you can coordinate the right tide and current conditions to times when the sun is low.

The tides, currents, winds, and waves not only dictate where the fish are likely to feed, but also work constantly on the ocean floor, bringing changes that can create or destroy good fishing spots in a matter of hours. A natural beach is a constantly changing piece of geography. Even those beaches where humans have altered the terrain with bulkheads, jetties, sea walls, and other devices, keep moving with little regard for attempts to change their courses. Some beaches grow while others are eroded away. The littoral drift carries tons of sand from one place only to deposit it in another. This process continues day and night and only a major storm that completely alters the coastline can change the process.

The most severe storms occur during the fall and spring, when big northeasters move along the coast following the passage of cold fronts. Occasionally, conditions are right for one of these storms to stay in an area for a day or two, and each new tidal change will flood the beach, cutting new inlets, building sandbars, and scouring out troughs. By the time the storm moves away you will have an entirely new beach, whose characteristics must be learned in order to uncover sites where fish are likely to gather.

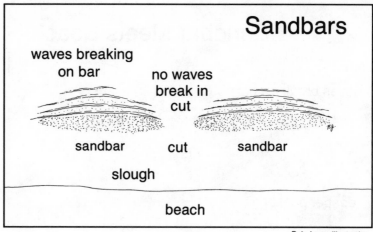

Structure

Anything that directs water flow can be classified as structure: a sandbar that breaks waves before they reach the beach; a deep hole that fills on the flood and empties on the ebb; a narrow but deep slough along the beach that channels water, bait, and game fish within range of your cast; a rock jetty that holds sand on one side but is washed away on the other will attract game fish that lurk on the deep side waiting for bait to be washed to them. Recognizing structure and being able to fish it correctly is one of the most important skills a surf fisherman can develop.

Sandbars

Sandbars are the most common type of structure found along the beach. They can run for miles off the beach or they may run close to shore. No matter where they are or how big they may be, you can bet they will attract some fish looking for shelter and an easy meal.

When surf casters talk about reading the beach they are referring to the ability to look at breaking wave patterns to determine where they would most likely catch a fish. The structure these waves break over are sandbars. A wave will break when the water below it is one-and-a-half times as deep as the height of the wave. In other words, waves break

WHERE TO FISH   95

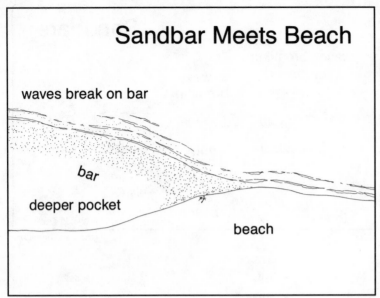

Sandbar Meets Beach

waves break on bar

bar

deeper pocket

beach

Bob Jones illustration.

over shallow water and not over holes, breaks, or sloughs where the water is deep.

As you look at the beach you will see the waves breaking in one place but not in another. The line of breaking waves indicates a sandbar, and those places where that line is broken by areas of waves that do *not* break indicates an opening in the bar. This is a classic place to fish. The opening provides a pathway for both game fish and bait to move inside the bar. A bait or lure placed around this break will intercept all types of fish, from croaker to channel bass.

The slough or trough formed between the bar and the beach can be quite deep. Depending on the shape of the bar and how far it runs offshore, these sloughs may form little lakes that will support a variety of marine life. Species such as weakfish, speckled trout, spot, and king whiting will take up residence in these lakes, providing steady action for bottom fishers. The real excitement occurs during the fall when schools of big bluefish move into these ponds to feed on the resident fish.

When the sandbar runs for a long distance without a break you may find fish holding tight to the inside edge. They will lie on or near the bottom, waiting for food to be washed down to them by the action

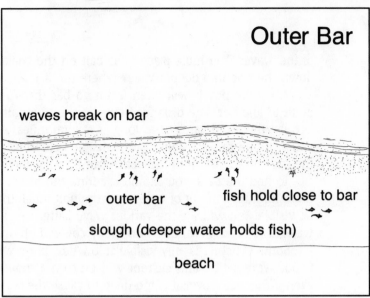

Outer Bar

waves break on bar

outer bar

fish hold close to bar

slough (deeper water holds fish)

beach

Bob Jones illustration.

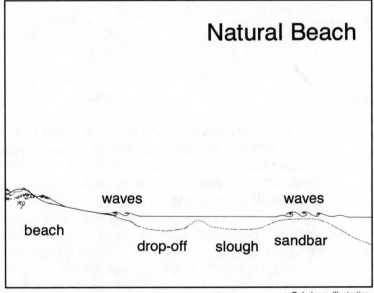

Natural Beach

waves

waves

beach

drop-off   slough   sandbar

Bob Jones illustration.

of the waves. You must place your bait on the bar and then let it roll down the side into deeper water where the fish are waiting.

A natural beach will often feature a bar that runs from one small point to another. The distance between the two points can be as short as a few hundred yards or as long as several miles. Along this distance you will find breaks, sloughs, troughs, and run-outs. The points where the bar comes back into the beach can be very good on high water.

To find the bars, you should examine the beach on low tide. With the minimum amount of water over the bottom all the structure should be visible. You will see the various wave patterns, color changes in the water, and exposed sandbars normally covered up on high water.

Some structure is only visible at low tide, but it will hold fish on the flood. Wave action and current will play on a mound of bottom sand even if the water over it is too deep to cause the wave to break. These little drop-offs can be hard to find, but they will hold bottom feeders such as flounder. When you begin to catch fish in one particular location along an otherwise smooth beach, chances are a small bar or mound has created a drop-off.

The vast majority of beach fishing structure is related to a sandbar. The points, capes, spits, bars, and drop-offs were all created when waves mixed with current and tide to move sand around and form it into many different faces. Your job as a surf caster is to recognize each face and fish it accordingly.

Points

Points, like sandbars, can vary in size and location. The best ones occur where two opposing currents meet, creating turbulence that washes bait into the mouths of waiting fish. These are very unstable structures. Any northeast blow will change them and a big northeaster can alter them completely.

The most famous point along the Atlantic Coast is on Hatteras Island. When a surf caster speaks of "The Point," this is the one he is referring to: the cold Labrador Current collides with the warm Gulf Stream, creating a violent piece of water known as Diamond Shoals. The place where Diamond Shoals meets the beach is known as The

Point. When it is really cooking, the force of the waves colliding against one another and with the shoals sends water and spray 50 feet into the air. The beach on the south side of The Point is quite steep, while the north side tapers out on a more gradual basis. A southwest wind brings big red drum and bluefish within range of surf casters and on a warm fall night the activity can only be described as chaotic.

Other famous points along our coast include Race Point on Cape Cod, Montauk Point on Long Island, Cape Henlopen in Delaware, and False Point at Cape Hatteras. Not every point is as big or as famous as these. Some develop along the beach where sandbars come into shore. Jetties, or "groins," produce the same types of structure as do points because the littoral drift washes sand away from one side while building it up along the other.

One of my favorite points is on Hog Island in Virginia. This ever-shifting piece of sand has produced more red drum for me than has the famous Point on Cape Hatteras, and without the hassle from competing anglers. Each time I fish on Hog Island I have to find the point. Sometimes it is only a mile or so from the north end of the island, and at other times it has moved up to 3 miles south. This structure only runs out a few hundred yards, but the deep water on the north side holds fish even in low tide. As the tide rises, the drum move to the area and you can hook them in less than 3 feet of water.

This type of point will only develop on natural beaches where the waves are free to move the sand without interruptions from bulkheads, jetties, or other man-made structure. You can locate these points by looking for waves that break a long way out and roll in without building up again. This indicates an even bottom from the point where the waves break, on up to the beach. Waves that break on an outer bar and then re-form before breaking on the beach indicate deeper water between the bar and the beach.

A point will normally have deeper water on one side and this is where the bigger fish are likely to "hang out." They wait there for food to be washed down or, in the case of bluefish, they will herd bait into this dead end and have a feast.

You may find fish up on the bar during periods of high tide and occasionally they will be on the shallow side if the current is moving over the bar in that direction. As a general rule the deep water will be on the south side of the point, but each beach is different so it pays to check out the exact conditions where you plan to fish. For example,

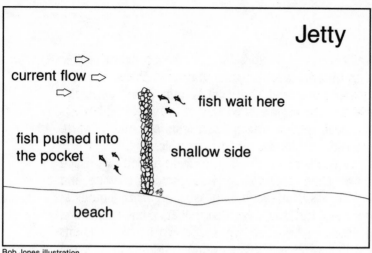

Bob Jones illustration.

the beach on Long Island runs east to west and the point on Cape Henlopen faces north.

Jetties

Jetty fishing is a subject that could be covered by a book all its own. The purpose here will be to describe how to fish from the beach around a jetty.

As mentioned before, jetties, or groins, are actually man-made points. They are placed along the beach to prevent erosion but the net result is *more* erosion on one side, and a buildup of sand on the other side.

Jetties are usually constructed of rocks, wooden pilings, sheet metal, or concrete slabs. Almost as soon as these materials hit the water marine life begins to grow on them. This attracts baitfish, which, in turn, attract game fish. The combination of a constant source of food and deep water close to the beach can produce constant fishing throughout the season.

Fish do not stray very far from a jetty. Striped bass, weakfish, sea bass, and tog will be found holding tight to this structure and lures or baits must be in or very close to the rocks.

Bluefish will use the jetties to ambush bait, either by driving the schools into the deep pockets on one side of the jetty or by working off

100   **SURF FISHING THE ATLANTIC COAST**

the down-tide side, waiting for the baitfish to wash past the end.

I believe there are more jetties per mile along the New Jersey shoreline than anywhere else on the East Coast. Consequently, anglers who fish this beach have developed jetty-fishing to the highest level possible. You can walk out on the longer structures, but many of the jetties are too small or too broken up to walk upon. Casting a swimming plug close along the rocks is a favored method of tempting weakfish and stripers to strike. Bommer, Rebel, Red Fins, Hellbenders, and Cordell plugs are favored. Sizes up to 7 inches seem to work best.

Bait fishermen use squid, crabs, or worms, and fish as close to the rocks as possible. They lose a few rigs, but sea bass and tog hate to move away from home so you must put dinner on their doorsteps.

The use of live baits such as bunker or herring from a Jersey jetty has resulted in more big striped bass than any other fishing method. Most of the men who pursue this type of action catch and store their own baits and treat each bunker or herring better than they treat their wives. The baits are carefully netted, then placed in a round live well until the time and tide are right for fishing. This is usually at night or in the early morning hours. Gently hooked through the nose and fished on 15- to 20-pound line without a leader, the baits are allowed to swim naturally away from the jetty. If casting is required it is done with great care.

Baits become quite nervous if big stripers are in the area and will try to escape by running to the surface. The big bass follow them up, often smashing them before eating. A long run-off usually follows the take before the hook is set.

Big bluefish, or "alligators" as they are affectionately known along this coast, can pose problems for the live-bait fisherman. When these fish are around, baits are usually gobbled up or cut in half before a bass can find it. After you spend all night standing waist-deep in cold water catching these baits, it is a little disheartening to see them disappear inside a bluefish's gullet.

Scalloped Beaches

If you look down a beach and see a pattern in the sand that resembles the scalloped edge of a pie crust, you are looking at a long row of little points. This type of structure seldom holds big fish but will frequently bring smaller specimens close to shore.

The scalloped design usually appears along a beach that does not have an outer bar. As each wave breaks directly on the beach it scours out little pockets, and at the end of each pocket is a small point. The wave action will often create turbulence on these points, stirring up baits such as sand crabs or worms, which in turn attract kingfish, spot, and flounder.

The mistake most surf fishermen make when fishing this type of beach is casting beyond the fish. You need to place your bait right at the end of, or close alongside, the points, and that may be only 25 to 30 yards from shore. Beyond this point there is no structure, and although you may find a passing bluefish or two, you won't have the more productive action available closer to shore.

As you look along a scalloped beach you will notice that all the points are not the same. Some will jut out farther into the water and may show a brown discoloration at the end. These are usually the best places to fish because the brown color indicates that the sand is being stirred by the wave action. A bait placed in this area should be well received.

Inlets

Inlets are narrow cuts through the beach where bays, rivers, creeks, or other bodies of water flow out to the ocean. Many of these inlets are protected with man-made structure such as rock or cement jetties. A few are still in their natural state and are subject to radical changes as tides, currents, and storms move them about.

There are certain characteristics common to all inlets, whether protected or not. There will be a deep channel leading from the ocean to the bay or creek. This channel will become a highway for bait and game fish, making it a very attractive place to place a bait or lure.

Current is the controlling factor when you are fishing an inlet. It moves the bait to the game fish and they take up stations at either end of the inlet, depending on the direction of the current.

Fish will feed on the inside of the inlet when the current is moving in and on the outside or ocean side when the current is running out. Please keep in mind that current and tide are two different things—

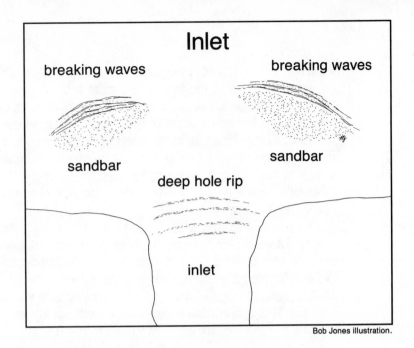

Bob Jones illustration.

similar but different. *Tides* are the rising and falling of the water level and *currents* control the direction—north, south, in, out—that the water moves toward or away from.

The current or water direction at an inlet is commonly referred to as moving either in or out. This can be confusing because the tides are also said to be moving in or out. If you can picture the rise and fall of the tide instead of it coming in or out, this may help clarify the situation.

When you check the tide table for the inlet you plan to fish, you may see a high tide at noon. When you get there at noon the water passing through the inlet appears to be moving in when your chart says it should be going out. What you are looking at is the current, which will continue to move in for a period of time after the tide has started to fall. How long the current will run against the tide depends on how big a body of water lies behind the inlet. The large inland bays found in back of most barrier islands along the East Coast take quite a long time to empty and fill through their inlets. Most current changes in these locations run two hours later than do the tide changes. In our example the current would change direction at 2:00 P.M., two hours after the high tide at noon. Each inlet is different and it often takes some personal observation and calculation to determine when the current changes will occur at the inlet you plan to fish.

There is a period of slack water between each change in current direction and the speed of the current gradually slows down as the time for change approaches. In some inlets the maximum current velocity is so fast you can't keep a bait on the bottom and working any type of lure is next to impossible during periods of maximum flow. Your best fishing times will be the two hours or so from the tide change to the current change as the flow drops off.

As you look at an inlet you will probably see areas where the water is very rough. There may be standing waves on the ocean side when the current is moving out and a similar but less dramatic wave action on the inside during periods of incoming current. These "rips" are the feeding zones for game fish and the place where you must put your offering. This is one time where "close" will not count: you either put your bait in the feeding zone or you go without fish.

I can vividly recall a day at Indian River Inlet when the blues were working baitfish in the rip between the bridge and the Coast Guard station. My fishing companion, Jeff Fink, as well as everyone else along the inlet, was able to get his lure out to the action while mine consistently fell 10 to 15 feet short. Jeff put seven or eight blues in the cooler; I went fishless. My problem was too light a lure and too heavy a line. We had been fishing from a boat and were on our way home from the marina when we happened upon the bluefish blitz. My boat rod was not set up properly for fishing the inlet.

Seeing a rip and getting to it can be two entirely different problems. The inside rips are usually accessible from the beach or from the jetty but the outside rips may be impossible to reach. Sandbars may form at some inlets, giving you access to the outside rip during periods of low water. The same situation will occur where jetties protect the inlet but are covered with water at high tide.

You must exercise caution on these bars and jetties if you venture out on low tide. Don't get so involved in your fishing that you fail to notice when the tide begins to rise. You won't be the first fisherman who has to swim back to shore, but that will not make the situation any less embarrassing. This situation can be dangerous in the spring and fall when the water is cold or during times when the seas are running high. I have seen fishermen washed into the inlet when a big wave broke over them. Lives can be lost when this happens, so it pays to keep an eye on the tide as well as the current.

It is quite difficult to fish bait in a rip. The vast majority of fish taken from this type of water falls to lures, but exactly what type of lure to use and when to use it can be a problem.

When the fish are obviously feeding on the surface, a top-water plug will produce exciting strikes. Work it fast on the down-current side of the rip. A floating lure can increase your casting distance. You can toss it into the rip and let the current carry it past the feeding zone before you begin your retrieve. In some situations you may not have to bring the plug back in and cast again if you don't get a strike. Just get it back to the rip and let it drift over the feeding zone again.

Fishing a surface plug is fun, but when the fish are feeding deep it won't draw their interest. This is the time for metal lures, jigs, or deep-diving plugs. Of the three, I prefer metal. These lures cast like bullets, sink like stones, and can be worked at different depths depending on the speed of your retrieve. Some metal jigs will cast well and sink fast but they don't have the action of a Hopkins or KastMaster. You can put a rubber tube or worm on the jig, which is often quite effective on weakfish and striped bass.

Bucktails are favored by many who fish around inlets. Although not ideal for working rips, they are perfect for fishing in close to shore where flounder and other bottom feeders love to lurk.

Inlets that are protected by rock jetties will hold many fish in close. Big weakfish and striped bass will live in this structure and a well-placed bucktail can attract their attention. This is another instance when close won't count. The bucktail must work in the rocks and if you don't lose one now and again you aren't getting the lure where the fish are feeding.

Swimming plugs can also be effective at inlets but they normally work best at night during periods of reduced current flow. Darters will work in a rip in similar fashion to a surface plug. Cast out, let the plug float through the rip, and work it back very slowly. A darter will work well with little more pressure than that supplied by the current.

Deep-diving plugs can be used at the inlets but they do have a tendency to hang up on the bottom. This usually occurs at the end of the retrieve as they move toward the shallow water close to shore. If your inlet has a steep slope and the bottom is clear of rocks or other hazards, you may find that a deep-running plug will pull some fish out of the rip.

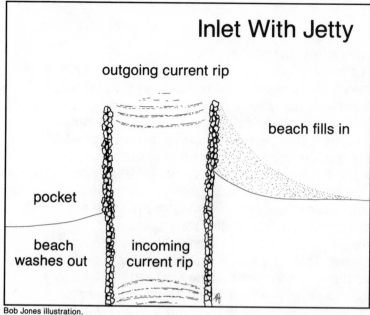

Inlet With Jetty

outgoing current rip

beach fills in

pocket

beach
washes out

incoming
current rip

Bob Jones illustration.

Depending on how the inlet is constructed, you can fish baits in close to shore or place them at the down-current side of the rips. Rocks and other riprap around an inlet are best fished by dropping your bait directly over them. Casting into such structure will eventually result in lost bottom rigs as the current pushes your hook and sinker into cracks and crevices.

Sandy-shored inlets can be fished like any other beach. Cast out and slowly retrieve your bait until you find the fish.

Putting a bait at the end of a rip is easier said than done. Many of these locations are so far from shore you can't reach them, while others have strong current flows that wash your bait out of the feeding zone before a fish can find it. If the rip is within casting distance and the current is not too fast, you should place your bait down from the rip where bottom-feeding fish are likely to find it. Channel bass will often inhabit these locations, feeding on baits washed out by the current.

Inlets are probably the single most productive fish-holding structure along the beach. It takes time to develop the technique required to fish them successfully but the end result is well worth the effort.

Rocks, Wrecks, and Other Structure

Anything that diverts water flow and creates turbulence along the beach has the potential of holding fish. If this structure also holds marine growth that brings in baitfish, so much the better. Rocks and wrecks do both jobs quite well. Some parts of the Atlantic Coast are littered with rocks left by the glaciers as they retreated north. The New England area is famous for its rocky beaches and these rocks not only attract tourists but also attract fish.

Most game fish use the larger rocks to ambush baitfish. They stay down current of the rock, where it takes less energy to maintain their positions and wait for food to move past. When they spy something they would like to eat, they dart out and grab it. You should work your lure or bait in such a manner that it passes close by the rock and gets some attention from the fish. This requires an accurate cast. If you get your presentation too close you may spook the fish or hang up on the rock; too far away and the fish will never know you were there. Lay it right above the rock and slowly work it past as if the current were washing a helpless morsel right into the mouth of that waiting fish.

A beach covered with smaller rocks will seldom hold fish in one specific location. Instead, they will move about in the same way they would over a smooth sand bottom. The advantage here is the rocks' ability to attract marine life such as grass and shellfish that in turn attract bait and game fish.

Baits such as worms, clams, mussels, and live minnows placed in the rocks work very well. Many anglers who fish this type of bottom use a flat sinker that doesn't hang up in the rocks quite as quickly as will a pyramid. They also tie their sinkers on with a light piece of line so that when it does hang up they can break it off without losing the whole rig or their fish.

Swimming plugs are very effective when worked over rocky bottoms. As is usually the case, nighttime or the hours at dawn and sunset are the most productive periods. An on-shore wind will often bring big fish in too, and create the turbulence around the rocks that stirs up the baitfish. These are ideal conditions for working a big swimmer or needlefish.

Shipwrecks close to the beach work the same magic as do big rocks. The fish hide in the wreck and wait for a passing meal; keep your lure or bait close to the structure if you want to attract their interest.

A large wreck will often have a deep hole on one side and a shallow area on the other. These structures are quite similar to jetties or points, and the littoral drift will scour out one side and build up a sandbar against the opposite end.

Red drum, striped bass, and big flounder will lie in the deep holes while sea bass, tog, spot, and other smaller fish work in and out of the wreck. Small baits and light tackle can be used to catch the small fish and these in turn can be employed as baits on heavier tackle to lure the big fish out of their holes.

The Boiler Wreck on Pea Island at Cape Hatteras has been there so long that it has developed into a permanent sand point with a deep slough running north toward Oregon Inlet. This is one of the premiere fishing spots along the Outer Banks and even though the Park Service provides parking lots you will see cars lining the road when the big blues invade this slough.

A pier is another man-made structure that attracts and holds game fish. Most of the coastal piers are built to provide access for fishermen who pay a fee to use them. Surf fishermen who work too close to the pier may find themselves the object of the pier owner's wrath. Although the beach is public domain and you can fish next to the pier if you choose to, common sense and courtesy are better served if you keep a reasonable distance from the structure. If you want to fish from a pier, pay the man and help yourself. (Note: In some states the law forbids fishing within 300 feet of a pier.)

As you travel along the Atlantic Coast you are likely to encounter many types of structure in the surf. Some of the barrier islands have washed away, leaving sod banks, forests, homes, and docks exposed to the surf. In fact, if the water level continues to rise we could have some very interesting structures in the surf at places such as Ocean City, Maryland, where large hotels and condominiums have been built on the beach.

As you develop your beach-reading ability you will see more and more structures and you will find more and more fish. Every place is unique but they all have similarities. Each surf-fishing trip should be a learning experience, but no matter how often you go, there will always be something new to see and a different set of circumstances to deal with.

The continuous changing of the tides, currents, weather, wind, and temperature keeps the beach and the fish who feed there in a constant state of flux. Your task as a surf fisher is to read the changes and react to them by knowing where the fish are likely to feed under the conditions that are present when you fish.

CHAPTER 6

RIGGING YOUR
BEACH BUGGY

Beach buggies became a popular mode of transportation for surf fishermen after World War II. Four-wheel-drive vehicles were available as war-surplus jeeps and some of the pre-War cars, such as Model-A Fords, were found to perform quite well on the beach.

Today the jeep is still around, but most of the Model-As are the prized possessions of collectors. While some surf fishermen use the modern equivalent of the Army jeep, the CJ-5, most have chosen the Cherokee due to the extra room these larger vehicles provide.

All the major United States automakers produce four-wheel-drive vehicles and many of the imported lines also have four-wheel-drive models. You can choose from big, roomy V-8s with every luxury option known to man, or pick a small four-cylinder economy model. The type of beach buggy you decide upon will be determined by your personal needs and taste. The man who always fishes alone and can afford a separate car for the family may be happy with a smaller, more personal vehicle. If you normally take some friends or your family up on the beach you will need more room. Those of us who own only one car that must see duty as everything from beach vehicle to chauffeured limousine will normally end up with a top-of-the-line four-wheel-drive, incorporating as many creature comforts as possible.

Until the 1980s, most of the beach buggies one saw were rigged as fishing machines with little thought given to any other purpose. They sported rod racks, cooler carriers, live-bait tanks, built-in tackle boxes, and were likely to have a favorite plug hanging from the rearview mirror.

Today's beach buggy is more adept at carrying groceries than fishing tackle. It is a midsize four-wheel-drive loaded with bogey boards, baby cribs, Brie cheese, and white wine. If BMW or Mercedes Benz made a four-wheel-drive wagon, people would buy it. If you searched real hard you might find a small box of rusted hooks and odd-sized sinkers hidden somewhere in the back. If they bothered to put a fishing rod on board it would probably be a spin-cast model bought on sale at K-Mart. These yuppie buggies proliferate in the summer but are replaced by genuine surf-fishing machines in the fall when tailgate parties replace beach parties on the social calendar. While many serious surf casters are less than pleased to find a group of party people camped at their favorite spots, they must remember that public beaches are open to the public and none of us hold exclusive rights to any part of the surf.

Unfortunately, there are some individuals and groups who would like to see all vehicles banned from the beach. They have preconceived notions that beach buggies are a threat to the environment when facts prove otherwise. In every impact study made to date that considered the results of four-wheel-drive vehicles on the beach, it was found that they did less damage than does foot traffic. The uncontrolled driving of four-wheel-drive vehicles over dunes or through salt marshes does cause severe problems, but surf fishers have no reason to be in these areas. The current trend among resource managers is to restrict all vehicular traffic to the beach between the toe of the dunes and the surf line. In some cases there is not enough room to run between the dune and the water so these beaches must be closed. In other areas you will find nesting colonies of seabirds, some of which are threatened or endangered, and to protect these animals the beach may be closed during the nesting season.

As this is written, surf fishers are holding their own against the protesters. Groups such as the United Mobile Sportfishermen have worked long and hard to keep the beaches open and we wish them continued success. It is in every surf fisher's interest to support beach-vehicle access. You may be assured that our enemies will turn their guns toward the walk-on angler if they ever rid the beach of vehicles. They won't be happy until all human intrusion is stopped.

Going under the assumption that we will be able to drive on the beach in the foreseeable future, let's look at some ideas on how to set

112

up your beach buggy. While we are assuming things, let's also assume that your four-wheel-drive vehicle will see other duties as well as fishing.

A surf-fishing beach buggy is nothing more than a rolling tackle box. You stuff it with all the junk you can't possibly fish without, even if you carried all your tackle in a 5-gallon bucket before you bought the four-wheel drive.

Surf rods pose the biggest storage problem. Two-piece rods can be carried inside the vehicle when not in use but those 10- to 12-foot one-piece sticks must ride outside. All of them will be carried outside while you are fishing, so some sort of rack must be devised for this purpose.

The simplest setup is a few pieces of 1½-to-2-inch PVC pipe clamped to a board and mounted on your bumper. The pipes should be 2 to 3 feet long with a bolt through the bottom to keep the rods from falling through. Although easy and inexpensive, this rig does have a few drawbacks. First, the rack is a semipermanent installation. This may be fine at the beach but your wife may find it less than attractive on "her" car when she meets friends for lunch or has to pick up her boss at the airport. Second, it serves only one purpose. You can't carry sand spikes, beach chairs, coolers, or other items that will fill your vehicle with sand if stowed inside. A carpet full of sand, fish slime, and bait takes on a life of its own and is especially appealing after the car has been locked up on a hot summer day. Finally, a simple rod rack is not practical for carrying one-piece rods over the highways. When carried in this manner the rods and reels are exposed to all the road dirt and bugs normally found on your grill and windshield. This abuse soon shows on the rods, which become chipped and pitted. Reels also suffer as dirt works its way into the drag mechanisms and gears.

A better solution to rod storage is a cooler rack with rod holders for beach use and a roof rack for transporting your rods on the road. You will find many variations of these items on the market or you can fashion them yourself. Depending on your skill as a carpenter, welder, pipe fitter, or metal worker, you can create some pretty fancy equipment. I have no skills in any of these areas, but I have managed to put together a cooler rack that was functional if not exactly a work of art.

I chose wood as the material for my cooler rack, using ¾-inch marine-grade plywood as the base. This is expensive stuff but I managed to come across a piece of scrap in a boat yard that was large enough for my purpose. It was 4 feet wide by 3 feet long and held my 86-quart

Igloo with room to spare. With a little careful loading I was also able to set a pair of beach chairs, my sand spikes, and waders on with the cooler. The liberal use of rubber shock cords keeps everything where it belongs.

A piece of one-by-six was attached to the front of the rack and carried six rod holders made from 1½-inch PVC pipe. The rest of the open space on the one-by-six was covered with license plates from the various surf-fishing clubs I belong to and the identifying plates and stickers that allow me access to the different beaches I fish. Each PVC piece was 2 feet long and secured to the rack with the proper-size galvanized pipe clamp. All screws and nails used to construct this project must be galvanized or stainless. Anything else will rust out while you watch. A pair of two-by-fours ran down each side of the carrier. I had several galvanized screw eyes set along these to accept the shock cords.

Now that we have a rack it must be attached to the vehicle. The most practical method I have found uses two pieces of galvanized pipe. One piece has a 1-inch outside diameter and the other has a 1-inch inside diameter. Weld two sections of the larger pipe to a convenient place on the under-carrier of your vehicle. These pieces are usually 12 to 18 inches long. Once they are secure, you can slip the smaller pipes inside, adjust them to fit the width of your cooler rack, and then attach them to the bottom of your rack with pipe clamps. To secure the smaller pipes inside the larger ones you can drill a hole through both and use a bolt or other fastener to hold them together. I used nothing but the friction between the two pipes and a shock cord attached to the bumper to hold my rack in place. It rode like that for ten years and was still there when I sold the car.

By using the pipes, you can easily remove the cooler rack when you aren't fishing. The pipes under the chassis are out of the way and seldom noticed by your non-fishing associates.

I have seen privately made cooler racks fashioned from various types of metal, but you can bet the folks who made these were metal workers by profession. If you have the necessary skills, equipment, and materials to make a rack from anodized aluminum or stainless steel, there is little I can add to guide you in this project.

Several commercial concerns manufacture cooler racks made out of metal. Some are local and only build on order but at least two of these companies have products available at tackle shops or by mail order:

Drill holes large enough to pass sand, scales, and other debris.

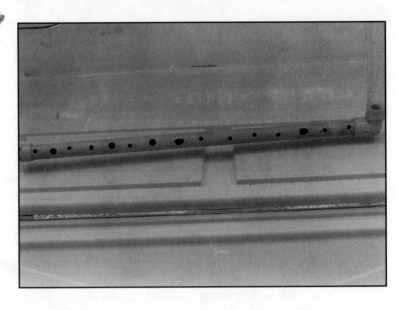

Hamburgers, 1501 Industrial Way North, Toms River, New Jersey 08753, makes cooler carriers, rod racks, sand spikes, and all the installation hardware needed to install these items. Let them know what size rack you want and the type of vehicle you plan to put it on and they will ship direct to your address. All of their products are made from aluminum, which is lighter than either wood or stainless. *Bob Lick,* 5 Mercury Avenue, Sewell, New Jersey 08080, makes his cooler racks out of stainless steel. He currently makes two sizes: one to fit 92-quart Igloos and another that will carry a 151-quart Igloo cooler. The smaller rack will carry six rods along the side and the larger one carries eight. Bob can arrange installation or you can have it installed at a local welding shop. My 1987 Dodge Ram Charger currently carries one of Bob's small cooler carriers. It is a bit heavy to move about but it is also very strong and I like the way stainless steel looks when it is all cleaned up and shiny.

Along some sections of the East Coast, cooler racks can become live-bait-tank carriers. The same cooler that held your squid and cold drinks during the summer can be converted to hold live bait for those big fish that move past in the fall. The conversion is quite simple and relatively inexpensive. All you need is a 350-to-450-gallon-per-hour bilge pump, a section of PVC pipe, a pipe clamp, and a piece of plastic hose to connect the pipe to the pump. You will also need some wire and a pair of clips to connect the pump to your battery. The PVC pipe must be set in a vise and have ¼- to ½-inch holes drilled 1 inch apart in a line down one side. These holes will let the water flow from the pump back into the tank. If they are too big the water will not be under enough pressure and it won't aerate the tank. Make the holes too small and they will clog up with sand and fish scales.

I hold the pipe in place by running two pieces of 40- to 50-pound monofilament fishing line through a couple of holes on each end and tying this around the hinges on the cooler. Other anglers elect to hold the pipe with clamps screwed to the back of the cooler. This is a permanent installation and because I use my cooler for purposes other than as a live well, I chose to go with a temporary setup.

You can also use an air pump to keep the bait alive. These pumps are driven by a belt connected to an electric motor and are usually installed under the hood of your vehicle. An air hose is run from the pump to your cooler, and this setup will keep more bait alive in a larger tank than will a recirculating live well. It also will put a greater drain on your battery.

I usually start my engine every hour or so when running the bilge pump. I let it charge for a few minutes, then I shut it off. I have gone for several hours without recharging and noticed no discernable drop in starting power.

Air pumps, on the other hand, can drop the charge of your battery to a low level rather quickly. How quickly depends on the size and age of your battery and on the outside temperature. A small, old battery won't last very long on a cold fall day. A deep-cycle battery installed for the purpose of running your pump might be a good idea if you plan to do a lot of live-bait fishing.

With your cooler used as a live well you now have a problem if you catch some fish you want to keep. I carry a smaller cooler in the back of the vehicle for just such an emergency. A few bags of ice are always in this cooler and any fish I want to keep will go right in on the ice. At the end of the day or night I can drain the live well, place the fish and ice cooler inside it, and not have the problem of a smelly fish box inside my vehicle. On those occasions when I don't want to dump the tank, I put the fish cooler in the vehicle only after I have cleaned off the fish slime and sand.

To make room for beach chairs, waders, sand spikes, and other such items, I had my rack installed with a good deal of space between the rack and the bumper. Chairs and sand spikes fit in here and are held in place with those ever-popular rubber shock cords. Waders are carried on top of the cooler, folded up and protected from chafing by a cotton rag placed between the shock cord and the waders.

Never drive along the beach or road with sinkers attached to your line. Remove them when you rack the rods to prevent damage to the rod finish or to the paint on your vehicle. You don't want a 6-ounce pyramid sinker banging around on your hood or breaking off and flying through the windshield. I put them in the cooler—on the bait board—and they are right there when I want to rig up again.

Rod racks for the top of your vehicle also come in a variety of shapes and sizes. Some cars have luggage carriers permanently mounted to the top and all you need to do is attach a suitable carrying device. In other cases where no permanent rack is available you will have to purchase a temporary one at the local auto store. These generally sit on rubber suction cups and are further secured by clips and straps that attach to your rain gutter.

My Ram Charger has neither a permanent rack nor a rain gutter, so I am forced to carry my one-piece rods on the cooler rack. Fortunately, they are old and beat up, so a few more nicks and bugs won't do much damage.

Devices used to hold the rods on the rack include ski carriers, clips, PVC pipes, and rod racks originally designed for boats. All do a good job when properly installed, but those lined with foam rubber do a better job of protecting your rods.

I have seen many surf fishermen riding down the road with both rods and reels secured to their roof rack. I suggest you remove the reel from the rod whenever you plan to transport them more than a few miles. The reels add weight to the load and I have seen them bounce off the roof of a vehicle when it hits a rough section of road. Reels are delicate pieces of machinery and you should try to keep them away from dust and dirt whenever possible.

All rod carriers should have a bolt or other such device through the bottom to prevent rods from falling through. When the reels are on, their handles will rest against the top of the rod carrier, which does prevent the rod from falling through but also takes a toll on the reels. Be certain your rod carriers are long enough to keep the rod inside when the going gets rough. A rod can bounce out of a short carrier and, no matter where it lands—on the hood, on the road, or on the beach—damage is certain to result. I recommend a carrier of at least 2 feet in length. You can cut a notch in the top for the reel handle: line this with foam tape or some other soft material to protect your reel.

Tackle storage is the next big problem facing the beach buggy owner. If your vehicle is used only for fishing, the solution is quite simple. Build custom racks and storage areas that suit your taste and the type of surf fishing you enjoy.

I knew a surf fisherman with a Chevy Blazer rigged with sleeping facilities for one person along the passenger side of the vehicle. There was a seat for the driver, and behind this he had built in a long cabinet-like affair that housed all his plugs, rigs, and other tackle. It also had a sink with a freshwater pump, a work bench with a vise and other tools, plus some drawers for his clean clothes. He could sit on the bed and brush his teeth, fix a plug, or change clothes. Everything was laid out to his personal specifications. Let me add that he was a young single guy who always fished alone.

Most of us will put our vehicles to other uses, and when we fish, it is usually with family or friends. We need to keep our tackle in a portable container and we need space left over in the vehicle for other people.

I have been using a Plano 747 tackle box for the past few years and I find it ideal for my beach buggy. It has three big drawers for plugs and a very roomy bottom compartment for rigs, sinkers, and a bunch of other essential stuff. Other people I fish with prefer to carry a few smaller boxes. One with bottom fishing equipment, one with plugs, and another with an assortment of odds and ends. Jerry Gomber from New Jersey built a wooden box that holds four of the flat Fenwick tackle boxes. This carrier has runners so that each tackle box can be removed, like a drawer, and a strap across the front to keep everything together when the vehicle is under way.

Claude Bain III from Virginia keeps all of his tackle in a 5-gallon bucket. He has cut holes and slots in the bucket to hold rigs, hooks, and lures. This also keeps the rigs from tangling with one another. Sinkers, leaders, bait, and his lunch all wind up in the bottom of the bucket. The one drawback to this system is a series of exposed hook points on the outside of the bucket. These invariably find their way into your waders or your hide.

Some surf fishermen rig lines on nets alongside the back windows of their rigs and hang their hooks and lures from there. This can be very convenient when you need to rig up in a hurry but won't do much for your image at the country club. It also leaves hooks exposed and they can often end up in places where they are unwelcome.

Everyone concerned is happier when your tackle is stored safely in an easily portable box. Plastic boxes don't rust and they won't melt rubber worms and other soft baits by contact.

Carrying natural baits in the family vehicle can lead to problems. The hauntingly sweet fragrance of overripe squid or the discovery of an escaped eel in the console can evoke unpleasant reactions by non-fishing family members.

A specific bait cooler with good hinges and a tight lid is the best insurance against most of these problems. I also keep a blanket over the floor of my vehicle just in case something does spill or crawls out of the cooler. Other anglers use a rubber mat or piece of plastic to insulate the carpet in their vehicle from such abuse.

You can carry your bait in the large cooler on the cooler rack or you can build a rack big enough to carry both containers. The wooden rack on my old Scout held a 68-quart fish cooler and a 28-quart bait cooler.

Food and drink should be carried in containers separate from bait and fish. I find one of those 12-quart personal coolers, such as the Coleman Oscar, a perfect way to keep half a dozen canned drinks and a sandwich or two fresh and cold.

As you shop for a four-wheel-drive vehicle, keep in mind that you will need storage space for all these fishing items. Pickup trucks have the maximum amount of storage but are limited in their ability to carry people. Some of the compact four-wheel-drives run on very little fuel but don't have a great deal of room for gear. Everything is a compromise, but don't sell yourself too short in any one area.

Other items to keep in mind when looking at four-wheel-drives include tires, shocks, cooling capacity, protection for the gear case and gas tank, as well as a finish that will hold up in the marine environment.

Tires are the single most important element to good handling on the beach. There are special tires made just for driving on the sand, but their tread is too smooth for road use. You will see other tires advertised as "Dune Busters" or some similar title. Just the name alone is enough to bring every tree-hugging preservationist out of the woodwork and down to the beach. I really can't blame them, because "dune busting" sounds as onerous to me as it does to anyone. These tires usually have a very deep radical tread that is better used in snow or mud. Tires that dig in are only going to get you into trouble up on the beach. Beach driving requires you to float over the sand, because if you start to dig down you will have to go quite a long way before you hit solid ground.

In my opinion, a set of high-quality steel-belted radial tires, just like the ones on your Cadillac, will do the best job on your four-wheel-drive. My original four-wheel-drive came with wide low-profile bias-belt tires. These were very popular on the muscle cars of the late sixties and early seventies. I was not dissatisfied with their performance. They had a wide footprint and fairly smooth tread. The lowest air pressure I had to run with them was 16 pounds on the beach at Cape Cod. When they finally wore out I replaced them with LR78-15 steel-belted radials. The first time I drove the new tires on the beach I thought I had bought a new vehicle. I never dropped the air pressure below 20 pounds on the beach and 32 pounds on the road.

Keep in mind that you will spend at least ninety percent of your driving time on the highway. If your tires don't perform well there they are going to cause safety problems and will probably wear out much sooner than you would like.

Your shock absorbers and suspension system must be hard. A soft suspension will cause the vehicle to buck and bounce in the sand and you won't set a good power transfer from the engine to the wheels.

This hard suspension can seem a bit rough when you make long highway trips. This is one of the trade-offs you make when you elect to use a four-wheel-drive vehicle for your family car. The ride may not be as smooth as that of a Mercedes, but you and your family are probably safer in a vehicle with a solid suspension that helps you keep control in a variety of different situations. Most four-wheel-drives also have greater visibility, are heavier, and have more passenger and cargo room than any family sedan on the road.

If you have a choice, you should equip your four-wheel-drive with the biggest cooling system available. These are usually part of the trailer package, because pulling a heavy weight behind your car may cause it to overheat. The same overheating problem will also occur as you plod along in deep sand on the beach. Driving 5 miles down Assateague

Island on a hot August day will put more strain on your cooling system than will pulling a 30-foot trailer up Pikes Peak. The trailer cooling package usually includes a larger radiator, a special transmission cooler, and may have additional oil capacity for the motor. All of these options are well worth the extra cost.

Shields for the transmission, transfer case, and gas tank are a good idea for any vehicle that will see off-road use. Some four-wheel-drive owners run through woods and streams where rocks and tree limbs create hazards. Beach fishers must contend with all sorts of debris that washes ashore. The most dangerous of this junk are the big wooden slats from pallets tossed overboard by freighter crews. They can lie buried in the sand, waiting for you to hit them with your tires, and then they jump up to do damage to your undercarriage.

Boards are not the only things that will mar the beauty of your pride and joy. Salt air, sand, and constant bombardment from ill-mannered sea gulls will take a toll on your vehicle's finish.

My Dodge Ram Charger has a 100,000 mile guarantee against rust-through. Other manufacturers offer similar guarantees. To help keep rust away you can choose from a variety of rust-inhibitive products that are applied to the undercarriage and to the finish.

Keeping your vehicle clean is very important. Wash it thoroughly after every trip to the beach. Rinse the undercarriage to remove salt deposits and sand. Remember, this sand carries salt and if left under your vehicle it will cause corrosion.

I wax my buggy twice a year, in the spring and fall. My wife vacuums out the carpet almost every week during the fishing season and pulls out a good deal of sand each time. Constant maintenance is the only way to keep your four-wheel-drive vehicle running right and looking good.

My old Scout was well maintained but the ravages of time in the salt air finally took its toll. I had the entire vehicle painted with DuPont Imron and this added another five or ten years to its life. A few spots were starting to show through when I sold it, but it would be another five years before any serious corrosion would require repair.

The way you drive on the beach can help you maintain your vehicle. The kinder you are to it, the longer it will serve you. Tire pressure must be lowered to accommodate the sand. If you insist on running with full pressure in your tires you will put a heavier strain on your drive train as it tries to turn your tires, which are digging into the sand. When you drop the air pressure, your tires begin to float on the sand because you have increased the surface area of the tread. This distributes the weight of the vehicle over a larger area and the tires are not as likely to dig in.

The softer the sand and the heavier the vehicle, the more air you will have to let out of your tires. My Ram Charger will run most beaches with 20 pounds of air in the steel-belted Goodyear Vector tires. The key is knowing when you are bogging down. If you need a lot of throttle to get going and maintain your speed you probably have too much air in your tires. If you end up digging yourself into a hole, the first thing you must do is drop the air pressure of your tires or else you will end up on the end of a tow rope.

You can let *too much* air out of the tires and this can be disastrous. When your tires are too low they can break the bead around the rim of the wheel, causing a complete loss of air. This condition is commonly referred to as a *flat tire.* Unfortunately, this is not as easy to fix on the beach as it is on the road. Bumper jacks are useless here because the sand won't allow a solid base for the jack. You should use a hydraulic jack placed on a board big enough to support the weight of your vehicle. You probably could raise your vehicle with a bumper jack, but even with the base sitting on a board I would still be concerned about the other three tires, which are on the sand.

A hydraulic jack doesn't have to raise itself nearly as high as a bumper jack does, which makes for safer operation. It will stow away in a very small area and can be used under a vehicle that has dropped down into the sand. Simply clear a hole deep enough for the jack and the board under the rear left spring or other suitable point.

Many public beaches require a complete list of equipment on board your vehicle before they will let you drive on the sand. This will vary slightly from one area to another, but a hydraulic jack and a suitable board are on almost every list. They also may require a tow rope or chain, shovel, and first aid kit. I carry a come-a-long, and some anglers have power winches attached to their vehicles. These devices will help you out of a hole if you can find something suitable to secure the other end. Since trees and rocks are a bit scarce on most beaches you will need another vehicle to use as a stanchion.

Caution and concentration are the watchwords when you drive on the beach. You must keep a sharp lookout for all sorts of debris that can puncture your tires, and be especially watchful for changes in the beach that could indicate soft sand.

One of the most serious hazards of beach driving is a wash-out under the sand. This happens when a pocket of water is trapped behind the berm and is running out below ground level. The beach can look fine, but when you drive across, the sand is literally washed out from under your wheels. The vehicle ends up on its frame and any attempts at digging it out will only push it in deeper. It will take a massive towing effort to remove any vehicle stuck in this soft, wet sand. The towing vehicles must be very careful or they could end up mired down along with the disabled four-wheel-drive. If you are ever stuck like this you will find out who your friends are. Don't waste time trying to free the vehicle yourself. Go for help immediately and notify the park rangers or other appropriate authorities as soon as possible. Many national seashore parks and state-maintained beaches have large sand-moving equipment that can also be used to remove beach buggies from the sand.

Most of the vehicles that get stuck on the beach dig their own graves. Too much air in the tires, tires that have too radical a tread design, and driving too close to the water account for the vast majority of driving problems.

If you do get stuck, and all of us do at one time or another, first lower the air pressure in your tires. Don't go below 18 pounds or you could run the tire off the rim. Next, get out your trusty shovel and clear the sand from the front and back of your tires. Remember, all four of your tires will be trying to dig out, not just the rear ones.

As you clean the sand, try to smooth out a track for 10 feet or more so that you can get up some momentum before you hit soft sand again. If the track is harder or runs downhill behind the vehicle, smooth your sand down in that direction. Getting unstuck is more important than moving ahead. The critical thing is movement, direction is secondary.

Trying to power out of a stuck situation will only get you deeper into trouble. A slow application of the throttle will give you a much better chance of moving ahead. Don't forget to fill up any holes you make. The next vehicle down the beach will really appreciate your thoughtfulness.

Most beaches have very soft sand at the water's edge. All of those TV commercials where the car is sailing along through the surf, tossing spray over the windshield, must have been filmed on Daytona Beach. Don't try it at Cape Cod, Assateague, or Cape Hatteras. I have seen vehicles sunk in the surf on every one of those beaches.

Running in the tracks left by other vehicles is a good way to avoid trouble. It can be a bit tricky if your tires don't exactly fit into the track, however. After fifteen years of driving on the beach I came to the conclusion that an International Scout has a track unlike any other vehicle.

If you are following a track that suddenly disappears, this would be a good time to stop. Get out and take a closer look. Sometimes it only seems to disappear because the sand is much harder in this area. In fact tracks that suddenly get very deep are more of a danger sign than are treads that disappear.

In any event, when in doubt about the surface of the beach, get out and walk the area. It is much better for you to sink up to your knees than to have your vehicle stuck down to the frame.

Another danger for beach drivers is wash-outs. These are very steep cuts in the beach, caused when water runs out of small sloughs created during periods of high tides. The cuts are often very narrow but can be 2 or 3 feet deep. They are difficult to see during the day and almost impossible to see at night.

Hitting one of these cuts will not only get you very stuck, but can also cause serious injury to the occupants of your vehicle and damage the front end. Most wash-outs occur below the high-tide line. If you stay above this line you will seldom encounter this hazard. Of course, when the tide is out the lower beach can be very smooth and hard, so most of us will drive down there. When you do, be very careful and don't be lulled into a false sense of security because the going is so easy.

Excessive speed cannot be tolerated on any beach. There is no excuse for driving faster than 25 miles per hour, and most of the time I run between 10 and 15 miles per hour. Anything faster than that will endanger you and everyone else on the beach. It will get you into trouble before you can avoid it and bring the wrath of every surf fisher on the beach down on your head. If you are spotted by a park ranger it will also bring a fine and the loss of your beach-driving privileges.

Most four-wheel-drive vehicles have two-speed transfer cases. The low range of this transmission will get you through some pretty deep sand. Those vehicles with small engines may find driving in low range the best method for getting around on the beach. I ran my six-cylinder Scout in low all the time and it seldom bogged down. My V-8 Ram

Charger seems to have plenty of power and I haven't put it into low range so far.

Manual and automatic transmissions behave differently when driven on the beach. It takes a bit of experience to educate your feet to slip the clutch while applying the gas so that your wheels don't dig into the sand. I find that using the low range of the transfer case helps you overcome some problems with a manual transmission. Automatic transmissions have slip built in. If you apply the throttle gradually, the power will transfer to the wheels in an orderly fashion.

All this slipping of the clutch in a manual transmission, and the converter in an automatic transmission, will create heat. There is little you can do to cool a clutch, but having a transmission cooler will help your automatic.

Driving on the beach is a convenient way to get your fishing tackle to the surf. It is not difficult and by using some common sense you won't get into trouble. Remember to keep your speed down, stay on designated over-sand routes, don't drive on the dunes, and watch out for wildlife. By obeying these few rules you will help keep the beaches open for all of us.

CHAPTER 7

THE FISH

The surf along the Atlantic Coast can yield a wide variety of fish, everything from cod in New England to tarpon in Florida. Some species are much more common to the surf line than are others, and these are the fish we will target.

Although surf fishers seldom catch enough of any one species to make a dent in the overall population, this does not give us carte blanche to be fish hogs when the occasion arises. Conservation must be the overriding force behind the actions of all who use the marine resource. At this writing only the striped bass, snook, and red drum are protected by bag limits and seasons, but some other species such as weakfish, speckled sea trout, and summer flounder do have minimum-size restrictions in some states. You must obey the law for the jurisdiction you fish, but I suggest you go further than that by establishing personal bag limits and releasing all fish that you don't need for food. Even though generosity is a virtue, it can be an excuse for overkill by those who try to feed fish to their entire neighborhoods.

Tagging programs are offered by the National Marine Fishery Service and the American Litatorial Society. Get involved with this work and you can help science learn more about the fish you like to catch. This knowledge can be used to manage the stocks, providing better fishing for everyone.

Bluefish

The bluefish (*Pomatomus saltatrix*) is found all along the Atlantic Coast, from Maine to Florida. While not as common in the northernmost part of its range as it is in the South, it is still the only species available to surf anglers throughout the region.

In my opinion, the bluefish is the epitome of sport fish. It grows to trophy size, it will hit almost any lure or bait you can name, and it fights with more power and ferocity than any fish that swims. My friend Russ Wilson claims it is harder *not* to catch blues than it is to catch them. There are times when his theory seems to be true, but most occasions call for some amount of skill if you want to score with bluefish.

The bluefish is a very well-equipped predator. He has excellent eyesight and a mouth full of sharp teeth. Add to this his ability to smell out baitfish or hear them through his lateral line, and you have a machine designed to hunt down and kill anything that doesn't kill him first.

Only the biggest and fastest of the pelagic species feed on blues. Bluefin tuna and mako sharks will take full-grown fish, and snappers are preyed upon by larger blues, weakfish, and summer flounder.

Blues tend to travel in large schools, but you will find stragglers along the beach, especially during the summer. They like a water temperature range of 50 to 84 degrees but seem to feed best when the temperature is around 70 degrees.

You will find them in the southern surf from Cape Hatteras to Florida during the winter and they move up the coast as waters warm in the spring. Maine may see some blues by August before they start back south in the fall.

During these migrations, large schools of blues will hit the beaches in what is commonly referred to as a *blitz*. A blitz can last for an hour or for a week. Most fall into the shorter time span but under the right weather conditions I have seen those fish stick in one section of beach for days at a time.

When a blitz occurs, Mr. Wilson's observation appears to be valid. Anything that hits the water will be attacked and there have been some reports from Florida indicating that blues have bitten swimmers. One must assume these victims were Midwest snowbirds who had never been introduced to the bluefish. Most of us who end up bitten by a bluefish received our wounds after the fish was caught. Blues die hard and can jump up to bite you even after they have been on the beach for quite a while. Their frantic twisting and jumping after they are landed can also inflict injury by sticking the angler with his own hooks. This is especially true when plugs loaded with three sets of big treble hooks are used.

A bluefish must be treated with care and respect whether in or out of the water. Don't try to remove your rig or plug until the fish is absolutely dead. If you want to release a big blue, the only safe way to do it is to cut the leader and let him go with the hook still in his jaw. Plug fishermen won't let a ten-dollar lure go, so they either have to remove the plug with great care or keep the fish.

But before you can release or keep a bluefish you must catch a bluefish. Since every day at the beach does not see a blitz it may take some work to put a blue on your hook.

All the various types of beach structure are likely to attract bluefish. They roam the coast looking for food, and if the structure holds bait, a bluefish will probably stop by. Soaking a bait is the most productive method to intercept a blue as he moves past. Mullet, spot, pinfish, squid, and just about any other type of bait you can name will get the blue's attention.

Live baits will attract blues, but they often hit the part without the hook. Stingers or two-hook rigs can help, but you will still miss a good portion of your strikes on live baits.

A Stinger is a treble hook on a short wire leader that hangs from the main hook but may not be attached to the bait. Its job is to snag a big blue or king mackerel as the fish attacks the live bait. This is not in the best tradition of sport fishing but it is used with some effect, especially along the southern beaches.

Not all blues are big, and snappers invade the beaches during the summer. Here too, cut bait is the way to fish. When the blues are really small, 1 or 2 pounds, a two-hook rig can be employed. Once the general size of the fish is over 5 pounds I would recommend a single-hook rig. Two bluefish of that size or larger on line at the same time is really not much fun.

Plugs and metal lures are very effective on bluefish. Poppers produce the most exciting strikes but metal or swimmers require less work to use.

Rips will hold bluefish during a running tide. Work your lure along the edge of the rip or drop your bait where the rip begins to slow down.

Any type of slough can be a feeding trough for bluefish. They will push bait to one end of the slough and occasionally chase their food out of the water and onto the sand. I have seen blues flopping on the beach after a receding wave left them stranded. You will also find weakfish, kingfish, and other such game fish left high and dry in their efforts to escape a school of hungry blues.

Movement can improve the chances of a bluefish finding your bait. They rely on their hearing and sight to locate most of their food, so slowly dragging the bait over the bottom can get their attention.

Plugs that move with a quick motion or create a disturbance on the surface draw more bluefish strikes than do slower-moving lures. The blue seems to feel challenged by anything that is trying to get away and he will make every effort to stop it.

Blues don't grab a bait, they chop it. If it is a big bait, they will cut it in half with one bite, swallow the part in their mouth, and let the other half fall away. Another blue may take the uneaten half or it may fall to the bottom where less-aggressive species, such as weakfish or striped bass, are waiting for an easy meal.

All bluefish baits and lures should have hooks placed fore, aft, and amidships. If you put your hook in only one part of the bait, the bluefish will eat the other part.

Don't forget to use wire leader on your baited hooks and as added insurance on your lures. There will be times when a wire leader will spook a blue away from a lure, and when this occurs heavy mono leaders will be the solution. You will probably lose a few lures but you will also catch some fish.

Landing a big blue in the surf will require a gaff. You may be able to pull him through a calm surf but any type of wave action will work with the fish, causing broken lines and straightened hooks.

Many people do not find the bluefish to be good table fare. I like them if they have been properly cared for and cleaned. Ice your fish as soon as you catch it, and clean it as soon as possible. All bluefish should be filleted and skinned. The bigger specimens should have the dark meat along the lateral line removed.

Once they're cleaned you can bake, fry, broil, or poach them. Many of us like a spicy bluefish recipe with lots of Old Bay, tomatoes, onions, and peppers all over the fillets.

Blues do not last very long in the freezer. They have a lot of oil in their flesh and this will break down after a month or two. Don't keep more blues than you can eat in the next few weeks.

Bob Lick with a 38-pound striper that hit a bottle plug on the North Bar at Montauk.

Striped Bass

The striped bass (*Morone saxatilis*) is the trophy fish of the Northeast Coast. It is currently in serious trouble throughout its range due to habitat destruction, pollution, and overfishing. The current restrictions placed on the catching and selling of this fish seem to be effective. The population in the Hudson and Delaware rivers has improved, but the overall picture in the Chesapeake Bay is still quite dismal.

No one can predict when we will have striper fishing again at the level we enjoyed from the late 1950s into the 1970s. Some don't believe we will ever have the stocks back to that level, but others are more optimistic. All the surf fisher can do is obey local laws and release fish unharmed.

Catching striped bass, or "rockfish" as they are called in my native Delaware, was never one of my greatest accomplishments. I spent many fruitless hours during the peak of the rockfish population cycle while all those around me landed fish.

There are probably more articles and books written on the various techniques you can employ to catch a striped bass than about any other saltwater fish. I have read most of them and tried everything they recommended but the striper continues to elude all of my efforts.

I think the one trait all good striper fishermen possess is persistence. They stay at it no matter the time of day, no matter the weather, and no matter what other social or business obligations fall by the wayside. Success with striped bass demands that type of dedication.

Unlike bluefish, striped bass do not seem to be constantly on a feeding binge. Their meal times are closely related to the tides, and fishing the tides is a key element to catching stripers.

Another way in which bass differ from blues is in their close association with structure. Blues will hang around a particular structure for short periods of time, while a big striper may stay around the same jetty or rip for an entire season. So long as the water temperature is within their tolerance—54 to 77 degrees with a range of 60 to 70 degrees preferred—and the bait supply remains good, a rockfish is not likely to wander too far from home.

Striped bass dine on a wide variety of foods. Bunker, mullet, spot, flounder, small blues, and weakfish, along with anything else that swims by their hiding place. They will also eat crabs, shrimp, lobster, clams, mussels, and squid.

They may not be too picky about what they eat, but they are very lazy and they want their meals served at their doorsteps. In speaking with anglers more fortunate than myself, those who have caught big stripers on a somewhat regular basis emphasize the importance of putting the bait or lure where the striper can find it easily.

There will be occasions when rockfish will stage a bluefish-type blitz. I was fortunate to be present at one such event on Cape Cod at Race Point. The stripers were chasing bait in the wash and every cast of a popper or swimming plug produced a 10- to 15-pound fish. It was one of the most exciting and fun-filled evenings I have ever spent on the beach. I have heard stories about this same type of action with stripers of 40 to 60 pounds, but I was never fortunate enough to be there when it happened.

A striper may eat many things, but only a few baits and lures have been effective over the years. High on the list of baits is the live or rigged eel. A rigged eel is worked like a plug or other lure. Cast it out and slowly work it back.

Rigging the eel requires a lead swimming lip, which is hooked through the head of the salted eel. A leader tied to the lip and passed through the body and out of the vent carries a second hook.

Live eels are also worked, but the retrieve is even slower than with the rigged eel. The purpose of slowly bringing the eel back to the beach is twofold. First, you cover more ground where stripers may find your bait; second, a live eel will do irreparable damage to your line if allowed to swim freely about. Cranking them in keeps their noses pointed in the right direction.

Many striper fishermen prefer eels that are not too frisky. They may keep them in ice water or otherwise slow them down before putting them on hooks.

Hooking is normally done through the lips or the eyes. When a bass picks up your eel you must let him run until the bait has been turned and swallowed. Strike too soon and you will put the bait out of his mouth. This procedure is true for most live baits, including bunker, herring, and spot.

Heavy leaders are seldom employed by live-bait striper fishermen. Bass have an uncanny ability to see a leader in the water and this will spook them away from the bait. Twenty-pound pink Ande line is the heaviest used in this type of fishing. It is tied directly to the hook—no snaps, swivels, or other hardware.

Worms are another favorite striper bait. When we had a spring run of rockfish along the Delaware Coast we used bloodworms to catch most of our fish. In New Jersey and points north the sandworm is also employed. Rockfish seem to prefer a big clump of worms on the hook with a nice long piece trailing away. This type of presentation can get

The Atom Junior is a great plug for all types of saltwater fish.

pretty expensive but that's what it takes to make a striper strike.

My favorite striper lure is the Atom Junior. This plug works in a slow side-to-side motion that seems to set stripers nuts. When rigged with an eel skin it looks like a big swimming snake. The eel skin is pulled on over the back of the lure after the trailing treble hooks are removed. It is secured to the body of the plug with cord or rubber band and the hooks at the middle of the plug are left in place.

Other well-known and effective striper lures include the Gibbs Bottle Plug, Darter, and Swimmer. The Creek Chub Pikie, Atom Striper Swiper, and the Danney plug have also taken their share of big bass.

While not a totally nocturnal pursuit, striper fishing is generally better after dark. This is especially true in the shallow waters of the surf where big fish feel exposed during the day.

The ideal beach structure for striper fishing has a point, jetty, or sandbar extending offshore with an area of calm water on the down-tide side. Big bass will lie in this calmer water, waiting for bait to be washed past by the current. Plugs and bait must be placed exactly on target so that they will work past the striper's nose as if they were struggling against the current. Doesn't sound too hard until you try it on a dark night, standing waist deep in a pounding surf with your hands stiff and numb from the cold. You can't see where your plug is going, you can't feel the line with your fingers, and you just had 5 gallons of

SURF FISHING THE ATLANTIC COAST

ice water wash inside your waders. Believe it or not, striper fishermen think this is lots of fun.

Taking all this abuse can pay off. Al McReynolds stood on an Atlantic City, New Jersey, beach on just such a night in 1982 and was rewarded for his efforts with a 78-pound 8-ounce striper that hit his Rebel Wind-Cheater plug. That fish stands as the current world-record holder.

Red Drum

If the striper is the big trophy fish for the Northeast surf caster, then the red drum, or channel bass (*Sciaenops ocellatus*), must hold that illustrious position in the Southeast. Found from Virginia to Florida, the channel bass spends most of his life in shallow water close to shore.

Channel bass tend to feed along the bottom something like a herd of cattle. They graze into the current, looking for crabs and small fish that they gobble up.

Drum don't have sharp teeth in their mouth but they do have a set of crushers in their throats. Because of this, they must swallow a bait in order to chew it. Sounds like a strange setup, but it works for the channel bass.

When a drum picks up a bait you should let him have it for a few seconds until he gets it situated in his mouth. Many fishers use a fish-finder rig so that the drum can move off with the bait without feeling the pressure of the line or the weight of the sinker. Exactly how far to let your fish run before you set the hook is more a matter of personal preference than anything else.

In some areas you may find red and black drum in the surf. The black drum is not a common catch by surf casters on any beach, but he does show up from time to time. The red drum is set apart from the black by one or more spots near his tail. Reds are also more of a copper color than are black drum, and they usually have slimmer bodies. Both fish feed on the same baits, both strike in the same manner, and both put up a dogged fight until they are landed.

There will be occasions when red and black drum will hit a lure. This is more common farther south, where smaller drum, called *puppies,* are the primary target. Those who fish the high surf in Virginia and North Carolina depend almost entirely on bait.

The author with a surf-caught black drum.

Lures such as big swimming plugs, Hopkins spoons, and leadheads with rubber tails will attract red drum. I have never had one hit a lure, but Claude Rogers of Virginia has pictures of both red and black drum taken on a Hopkins. Anglers who work the outer bars and inlets from boats have considerably more luck with artificials than do the beach fishers.

A variety of baits are used on drum. Mullet and spot are popular on Cape Hatteras. Shrimp are favored in Florida, and whole surf clams are used in some areas. Above all of these, in my opinion, is the peeler crab. I have used the other baits, but every red drum I ever hooked was taken on a peeler crab. The few red drum I kept for food all had crabs in their stomachs when dressed out. Crab is their natural food and therefore it makes the top bait.

Peeler crabs are not an inexpensive bait. I have paid as much as $1.50 each for them, but if they produce red drum I consider it a wise investment. Peelers do require special handling to keep them alive. They should be stored in eel grass or wet newspapers and kept as cold as possible in a cooler. Do not let them sink into the ice water or cover them with ice—that fresh water will ruin your bait in a very short time.

To use a peeler, remove the hard shell from the top of the crab to expose the soft crab inside. Turn it over on its back and cut into four or six pieces. Small peeler may yield only two baits, one out of each half. On larger baits you can divide the half into two or three sections.

Put the hook through a leg hole, not through the shell. This will help hold the bait on the hook. Some anglers will employ string, rubber bands, dental floss, and other such materials to hold a crab on the hook. I find a hook through a leg hole combined with a gentle cast works very well.

No matter what type of bait you use, you still need to set the hook to land the drum. They have very hard mouths, so sharp hooks are a must. When you use a fish-finder rig you need to get all the slack out of the line before you can drive the barb home. Do this by pointing the rod tip toward the area where the line goes into the water and cranking like crazy until the line comes tight. Immediately raise the rod tip and set the hook. If you suddenly feel as if your rig has snagged a southbound freight train, you are probably into a red drum.

You will find red drum in deep holes and sloughs where they often congregate to feed. I have seen them move across shallow areas during periods of high tide, but they generally prefer the edges of sandbars and channels. Drum are not afraid of rough water. You will find them working the bottom at inlets and on points where waves break with great force. This heavy wave action stirs the crabs and other food out of the sand or bunches up small baitfish so that the drum have easy pickings.

You must put your bait where these fish can find it. Sometimes this will require a long and accurate cast if the edge of the outer bar is 75 to 100 yards from shore. Other locations need only a short cast because the fish are up on a bar or there is a deep cut close to the beach. You can over-throw your fish just as easily as you can fail to reach them with your best cast.

Some red drum fishermen feel nighttime is the best for catching these fish. Others, like myself, have had more luck during the day. If the area is heavily fished or has a lot of boat traffic, night may be a better time. On the barrier islands of Virginia where fishing pressure and boat traffic are not a problem you can do just as well during daylight hours.

Cape Hatteras produces more big red drum than does any other stretch of beach. Many are taken at The Point, but the beach north of Avon also produces a good number of trophy fish. That is where Dave Deuel was fishing in November of 1984 when he took the current all-tackle world record 94-pound 6-ounce drum. Dave is a devoted surf fisherman and he has been rewarded with one of this sport's most coveted trophies. The chance of hooking an even bigger red drum keeps him, me, and a small army of other surf casters out on the beach.

Weakfish

The weakfish (*Cynoscion regalis*) is found along the Atlantic Coast from Massachusetts to Florida. In New England it is known as the *squeteague,* in Delaware and Maryland it is *sea trout,* and in the South it is a *gray trout.* All of these regional names can confuse the traveling surf fisher, but once you see a big weakfish fresh from the sea with its yellow fins and the purple glow from its head and back, you won't have any problem identifying it in the future.

The largest populations of weakfish occur around the Delaware and Chesapeake bays. The beaches of New Jersey, Delaware, Virginia, and North Carolina provide most of the surf-caught weakfish. Long Island, New York, had some excellent weakfish action in the late 1970s but it has fallen off dramatically by the mid-1980s. A good year or two could expand the population northward again sometime in the future.

Weakfish seem to travel in schools divided by size. The big fish, over 10 pounds, will arrive in the spring to breed in the bays, and when the spring is over they disperse to take up residence among rocks and other structure along the coast. Smaller fish arrive later, and after spawning they tend to remain in schools, feeding along channel edges and sandbars or over grass beds. They will move into the surf during the summer, but this is generally a nighttime activity.

We seldom get a shot at the big weakfish in the spring. They pass by the coast on their way to the bays before the water has reached the temperature level where they begin to feed. Even in the bays after the water has risen to 60 or 65 degrees it can be very difficult to catch these tide-runners.

The second assault by the smaller weakfish can be intercepted by beach fishers. Bloodworms are by far the best bait for these fish at this time of year. I have experienced days when weakfish were caught on every cast, but those are few and far between. The normal pattern is a little flurry of fish followed by a long lull.

In the summer, most weakfish are taken around jetties, piers, or other such structure. Live baits such as spot, squid, or crabs are captured by anglers using a cast net and immediately put on a hook and sent back into the water. Depending on the current, you may have to use some weight to encourage your bait to swim down to the weakfish, but in periods of slack water or in areas where the current is slow, live-lining an unweighted bait works best.

Bucktails and Mirro-Lures are two favorites of the jetty jockey. These weakfish are going to be in the rocks and your lure must go in after them. In New Jersey and New York a dropper fly is often placed ahead of the plug to imitate a baitfish being chased by a large predator. Strikes usually occur on the fly as the weakfish tries to steal the other guy's dinner.

Fall fishing is generally best for weakfish. The big tide-runners are heading south for the winter and they are on a feeding spree, storing up energy to carry them through the cold weather. The favorite food at this time of year is spot or mullet. These fish are also heading south and the weakfish plan their travel schedule to coincide with the migration of the spot and mullet.

Trying to figure out where and when these big weakfish are going to slow up can be a frustrating business. They are on the move and don't seem to hold in any one place for very long. My best catches have come from open beaches without any definitive structure. Some locations, like the Point at Cape Henlopen or the North Pocket at Indian River, often seem more productive than others, but this is due to the large quantities of bait that build up in these areas.

I have found that weakfish don't feed well when the surf is rough. A gentle east breeze or no breeze at all will create the optimum conditions for catching weakfish.

Generally, you will find weakfish more cooperative during the nighttime and just before dawn or at dusk. I have caught them at midday, but the angler who works after the sun sets will do much better.

Live bait is the key to success for big weakfish in the fall. The smaller specimens will hit cut bait and so will the big boys on occasion, but to catch them consistently a live spot or mullet on a fish-finder rig is the ticket. Use a 6/0 Beak-style hook on 2 or 3 feet of 40-pound leader ahead of your fish-finder. Connect the leader to your line with a snap to prevent the knot from jamming in the fish-finder sleeve. The bait can be hooked through the back, tail, lips, or through the eye sockets. I find the eye socket works best and creates less stress on the bait. It stays alive much longer and swims in a more natural manner.

Fish-finder rigs don't lend themselves to long-distance casting. Use a gentle, smooth motion and your bait will stay on the hook. You will be surprised at just how far you can cast using this method. Keep in mind that a long cast that fails to deliver the bait with the hook is seldom effective.

When a weakfish picks up your bait he will swim off as he turns it in his mouth before swallowing it, head-first. You must let him move away before you set the hook. Start with a slow count to five, crank out all of the slack, and then drive the hook home. If you miss the fish, increase the count to seven or eight and be certain to get all the slack out of the line before you try to set the hook.

I have tried various types of lures on weakfish when I knew they were in the surf, but to date I have not had much success. In New Jersey and New York surf fishers cast and retrieve a Diamond jig slowly across the bottom to catch weakfish. This technique probably works well along that portion of the coast because the weakfish are feeding on sand eels instead of the spot and mullet they are so fond of farther south.

I had one spectacular catch of weakfish at Fenwick Island, Delaware, on a mild November afternoon. Leonard Maull and I found a big school of weaks that inhaled our live spot before we could close the bails on our spinning reels. The two of us put forty-six weakfish between 8 and 12 pounds in our cooler over a three-hour period. We probably lost half again that many in the wash. I am a bit more conservative-minded now and limit my take to no more than ten fish a trip, but in 1980 it seemed like there was no end to the weakfish supply. Unfortunately, there was, but it appears they are making a comeback, which is good news for all saltwater anglers.

Spotted Sea Trout

The spotted sea trout (*Cynoscion nebulosus*), also known as a speckled sea trout, speck, or simply trout, is found along the southern part of the Atlantic Coast. It will occasionally show up on Assateague Island in Maryland but is much more common from Virginia to Florida.

My experience with specks has been on the Outer Banks of North Carolina in the fall, when they chase bait into deep holes or sloughs close to shore. The best of this fishing occurs when the wind is out of the west and the surf is fairly clean and calm.

According to Bill McCaskill at Whalebone Tackle in Nags Head, a Speck-Rig coupled with a pair of green Twister Tails makes an ideal lure for spotted sea trout. A Speck-Rig consists of two bucktails tied in tandem about 8 inches apart. Mirro-Lures are also popular with speck fishermen.

As you might have guessed from the small lures used on spotted sea trout, you won't be working with heavy surf rods and reels. A 7-foot spinning rod matched to a reel filled with 10- to 12-pound line is the ideal setup for this type of fishing.

Bait fishing will also produce speckled trout. Shrimp is a favorite offering, but I have caught them using squid, cut spot, and peeler crab.

Shallow water around grass beds is a natural home for speckled trout. While this is not the high surf, you will find many surf fishers who wade these flats, casting grubs and plugs or working with a live shrimp under a popping cork.

When spotted sea trout have bait bottled up in a hole or slough you can often detect their presence by the birds diving into the water to pick up stray pieces of bait. There will be times when the fish are feeding less aggressively and the only sign of this will be small swirls on the surface.

Most speck anglers will drive along the beach looking for holes and sloughs that might provide some action. When they encounter such a place they will stop and make a few exploring casts to test the waters. If nothing happens they soon pack up and move on. Another technique employed by less mobile fishermen is to find a likely looking hole and wait for the specks to come to you. Fish some bait on the bottom with a heavy rod while you cast a Speck Rig or other lure with your light tackle.

Although spotted sea trout do reach weights in excess of 10 pounds, most of those taken in the surf fall under that mark. This makes light-tackle fishing even more enjoyable because it matches the size of the catch.

The spotted sea trout is right up there with the channel bass as a trophy fish for southern surf casters. They are a beautiful fish that fights hard and makes a delicious meal.

Flounder

Surf fishers along the Atlantic Coast are likely to encounter three species of flounder: the summer flounder (*Paralichthys dentatus*), the southern flounder (*Paralichthys lethostigmus*), and the winter flounder (*Pseudopleuronectes americanus*). The summer flounder, or fluke, is quite similar to the southern flounder and their ranges do overlap in North Carolina. The color of the summer flounder is usually a darker brown with distinct spots, and the southern flounder is more an olive drab with diffused spots. Both of these fish are active predators sporting a mouthful of needle-sharp teeth. The winter flounder, on the other hand, has a round, soft, toothless mouth that it uses to suck worms out of the sand or mud. Winter flounder are right-eyed and southern and summer flounder are left-eyed. This means that if you put the winter flounder white-side-down, its eyes would be on your right as you look down on it.

Winter flounder are seldom caught south of New Jersey. In the late 1960s and early 1970s we had some good fishing for winter flounder in Delaware and Maryland during the spring. I have caught quite a few while fishing with bloodworms for stripers but I haven't heard of one taken along this stretch of beach for over ten years.

Worms, clams, and mussels are the top baits for winter flounder. As the name suggests, they frequent inshore water during the colder months and you can expect to catch them from November into March or April. In New England they can be taken during the summer due to the colder water temperatures along that section of coast. I have caught them on Cape Cod in early September when the scheduled appearance of some striped bass failed to materialize. We saved the trip by dunking bloodworms at the mouth of Sandwich Creek and putting some nice fat flounder in the cooler.

A long narrow hook, such as the Chestertown or Tru-Turn, works very well on winter flounder. Thread the hook through the worm and when the flounder sucks it in it will take hook and all.

Most winter flounder caught by rod and reel weigh less than 2 pounds. Larger specimens normally stay offshore in deep water, but occasionally they come in range of the surf caster. We hit a school of these bigger fish at Indian River Inlet in Delaware one spring day and while most of us were after rockfish we were more than happy with a half-dozen or so big flounder in our coolers.

Summer flounder and southern flounder are much more aggressive than is the winter flounder and will take a wide variety of lures and baits. I have caught them on cut mullet, live spot, squid, shrimp, crab, and shark belly. A white bucktail and a strip of squid is an excellent combination for these flounder when they are in shallow water. Other lures that take them include Hopkins spoons, Mirro-Lures, Stingsilvers, Speck-Rigs, and Diamond jigs. If it looks like a baitfish and you can work it across the bottom, a flounder will probably try to eat it.

Getting your bait or lure on the bottom and working very close to shore are the two key elements in successful surf fishing for flounder. One look at a flounder and you know it is not built for surface feeding. For some reason they seem to like the shallow waters between the breakers and the beach when looking for food. As an extreme example of how close to the beach a flounder will feed, I once caught one of about 2 pounds on a Hopkins lure hanging from the end of my 11½-foot surf rod. Since I was standing on the sand when the lure dropped into the water that flounder was less than 11 feet from shore.

I believe they lie along the drop created by the breaking waves and wait for bait to wash down to them. When you are casting lures for flounder the hit will often come just about the time you decide to pick the line up and cast again. For this reason it is a good idea to work your lure or bait right in to the beach.

Movement is very important in flounder fishing. You should cast out and slowly retrieve both baits and lures. Flounder like to ambush their food by lying on the bottom, covered with sand, and then pouncing on the victim as it passes by. They do move around a bit and may stumble across an anchored bait, but you will have more success if you bring the bait to them.

Since you want to move the bait across the bottom you don't want to use a pyramid sinker that will dig into the sand. I prefer a bank sinker and others choose a trolling or egg sinker. The exact type is not important so long as it will move easily over the bottom.

Move your rig in short hops. This will stir up the bottom a bit and may help attract the flounder's attention. Move the bait or lure a few feet, then stop for ten to fifteen seconds before moving it again. The fish will usually hit when the bait is stopped.

A flounder rig is tied so that the bait stays on the bottom. I use 30- or 40-pound leader material with a surgeon's loop tied on one end for the sinker, and a few inches above that I tie a dropper loop for the snelled hook. A fairly long leader of 18 inches to 2 feet is often employed to make sure the hook follows the sinker at a reasonable distance. You can add spinner blades, red beads, and bucktail hair to the leader as an added attraction. The extra weight from the blade and beads will help keep the bait on the bottom.

The English style, or wide-gap, hook has found some favor among flounder fishermen. It seems to hook and hold these fish quite well while some of the more conventional hooks pull right through their mouths.

One advantage to casting and retrieving your bait for flounder is that you are holding the rod in your hand rather than setting it out in a sand spike. You will feel more hits and catch more fish by tending to the rod personally.

Flounder seldom drive bait up on the beach and they don't school up for mass migration in the spring and fall, but they do provide a willing target for the surf caster throughout the season. The highest concentrations of flounder I have encountered were along the Outer Banks of North Carolina in the fall. Flounder are thought to spawn off this coast during the winter and I suspect they move into the surf to feed heavily before the reproduction cycle begins. Whatever the reason, you can find them all along the beach from Nags Head to Hatteras Inlet and most of these fish are well over the 13-inch length limit suggested by fishery managers.

Many people think the flounder is the best-tasting fish in the ocean. Proper filleting produces beautiful boneless strips of pure white meat that is great simply fried and eaten without further embellishment.

Others like to add crabmeat to the flounder and bake this into a scrumptious casserole. Although the flounder is a great eating fish, don't let your appetite overwhelm your conservation ethics. Don't take more than you can use and be sure you use all that you take.

Sharks

There is a growing fraternity of surf fishermen who deliberately set out to catch sharks. They rig up big conventional rods or spinning outfits and fish large hunks of bait on heavy-cable leaders in an attempt to wrestle "Jaws" to the beach.

Some shark anglers use baits so large they are impossible to cast. A volunteer is selected to carry the baits out to deep water, using anything from a surfboard to an inflatable boat or canoe. This is usually done at night and the boat has to be launched through the surf. My first thought when presented with this scenario was that, if there are sharks out there big enough to eat a 10- or 15-pound bluefish or take the head off a 60-pound tuna, what is to prevent this same shark from taking a nip out of the fool who is paddling the surfboard or boat? To date, I have not heard of anyone who encountered a shark while carrying the bait, but I will still leave this task to one who is younger and perhaps a bit less conservative than I.

A more conventional approach to shark fishing in the surf is to use a wire-leader rig similar to the bluefish rig, and a big chunk of cut bait. Whole baitfish will also work if they are not too big to cast. Hooks should be forged for extra strength. I would recommend 6/0 to 10/0 sizes, depending on the size of your bait and the size of the shark you hope to catch.

Night is the best time to catch a shark in the surf because they are more likely to cruise the shallow waters after sundown. Sharking is usually good in the hottest part of the summer when most other types of surf fishing are at their worst. These two factors combine to give us summertime sport in the surf. Another positive factor about sharking at night from the beach is the cool ocean breeze that develops even during the hottest time of the year.

The average size of a surf-caught shark is less than 25 pounds. Most of these will be sandbar or brown sharks, but other species do show up close to the beach: lemon sharks, blacktips, dusky sharks, and even hammerheads have been caught from the shore. Actually, almost any species of shark can move into the surf, including that terror of the sea, the great white shark.

Some shark anglers I have spoken with use a fish-finder rig so that the shark can move off with the bait before the hook is driven home. Others use a standard bottom rig and set the hook the moment the fish hits the bait. I suspect the fish-finder would work best with big baits for large sharks. It does take a bit of time for the fish to get the bait situated in his mouth and the hook in place for the strike. Smaller baits can be set up quickly because the shark usually takes them in one gulp.

You can expect a long dogged fight from most sharks. The blacktip will often leap clear of the water, but most other surf-caught species keep the fight on the bottom. This type of fight is best handled with a firm drag to let the shark know he is in trouble. If you set the drag too low he will simply swim away with all of your line.

Brown sharks are excellent table fare, but they must be cleaned as soon as they are caught. Remove the head and entrails and make sure you have cleaned the area around the backbone or cartilage thoroughly. This is where the kidneys are located and if they are left in you will have uric acid throughout the meat and it will be inedible.

It is usually much easier to tag and release a big shark than it is to land one. The National Marine Fishery Service (NMFS) will supply the tags and AFTCO makes a nice long tagging stick. Once the fish is in the wash, simply tag him behind the dorsal fin and cut the leader. The card you send back to NMFS asks for the type, sex, and size of the shark. This can be difficult information to collect on a dark beach, but with a little study beforehand you should have enough knowledge to identify the species and give the approximate size.

I become quite upset when I find a pile of dead sharks left on the beach by some slob fisherman. Not only is this a waste of the resource, but it also makes every other surf fisher look like a slob in the eyes of the general public. I don't care if they are dog sharks, skates, or bluefish—don't leave anything on the beach and return all unwanted fish to the ocean *alive*.

Bottom Fish

Bottom fishing is a broad term used to describe the practice of tossing out a piece of bait and waiting for something to eat it. Surf fishers spend a good deal of time doing this, most of it without any tangible result.

Most areas of the Atlantic Coast have certain species that are considered prime targets for bottom fishing. It may be cod or winter flounder in New England, king whiting or croaker along the mid-Atlantic, and pompano or spot Down South. These types of fish frequent the surf line for much longer periods of time than do the pelagic bluefish or the highly migrational channel bass, striper, or weakfish.

Catching bottom fish requires feeding them something they like to eat. Bloodworms for winter flounder and spot, shrimp for kingfish and small trout, and sandfleas (mole crabs) for pompano. Squid strips are a universal bait that will catch almost any bottom fish at one time or another.

If you set out to catch these fish you must begin to think about where they are likely to be. Since many small bottom fish end up as dinner for larger game fish it is unlikely that you will find them far from shore. Also, remember that these fish eat smaller fish, shellfish, and worms, which are stirred up by the wave action close to shore. If you are beginning to get the idea that bottom fish are seldom caught at the end of a 200-yard cast, you are absolutely correct.

Place your baits from the breakers to the beach. A cast that falls just behind the waves will put you in productive territory. If you want to increase your chances, slowly work the bait back to the beach as if you were fishing for flounder. Come to think of it, flounder are bottom fish too.

Small hooks—#2 to 2/0—and small baits work best for most bottom fish. As a rule, these fish have small underslung mouths and they tend to nibble or suck their food in rather than taking it with a vicious strike. Keep your leaders short, between 6 and 8 inches, to help you detect a gentle bite. Actually, your sinker buried in the sand will hook more of these small fish than will your rod because when the fish hits the bait and takes the hook he comes up tight on the short leader to the sinker long before you ever feel him through 50 or more yards of half-slack 17-pound line. Since an 8-ounce fish doesn't have much chance of pulling a 6-ounce sinker out of the sand, he ends up hooking himself.

A plain hook or one with only a small amount of bucktail hair or rubber skirt works best. Small floats can be used ahead of the hooks to add some movement to the baits. Some anglers think these floats will keep the crabs away from the bait. I have tossed out many such floats

Pompano are popular bottom fish in the southern surf.

Joe Malat photograph.

that were crushed to pieces in the claws of a blue crab.

Fish such as kings or winter flounder feed only on the bottom. If they are your target do not use any type of float on your hook. I like the sea mullet (as northern king whiting are known Down South) rigs sold in many southern tackle shops. They have two leaders with a small rubber skirt and a snap on the ends. You can clip a Chestertown or any other style of hook on with the snap and the rubber skirt adds motion to the bait while it keeps it on the bottom. I have used this rig with a wide-gap hook baited with cut mullet on one leader and a Chestertown hook baited with bloodworm on the other. The mullet will attract small blues, trout, or flounder, and the worm works well on kingfish, spot, and croaker.

Pompano are one of the most popular fish in our southern Atlantic surf. Sandfleas, or mole crabs, and shrimp are the best baits with clean water the ideal condition for catching these fish. You can get all the sandfleas you will ever need by sending a kid with a plastic shovel and pail down to the surf line and showing him or her how to dig up these little creatures. Kids are much better suited to this task than are grownups, for several reasons. First, they are built closer to the ground so they have less trouble getting up and down than we do; second, they have quick reflexes, which are required to capture a mole crab as he digs down into the soft wet sand; finally, kids don't mind getting wet or having a bathing suit full of sand. We hit the beach wearing waders, foul-weather gear, and long underwear, only to be greeted by a gang of kids playing in the surf. Kids and mole crabs were made for each other.

After you acquire your bait, impale it on a 1/0 to 2/0 hook and toss it just beyond the breakers. When the pompano are in good supply you may see them dashing through the waves looking for your sandflea. If you are fishing a beach with an outer bar the pompano will often cross it to feed in the slough when the tide is high.

Bottom fishing does not always produce the fish we were hoping to catch. Smooth dog sharks, skates, and sea robins are but three of the species that seem never to have a low population cycle. Larger dog sharks, if cleaned immediately, yield fine white fillets. I have heard that sea robins are good to eat but so far I have resisted this culinary delight. The old trick of using a cookie cutter to punch out scalloplike pieces from a skate's wings is more widely talked about than practiced. Generally these and other so-called trash fish should be released alive. Just because we don't want them does not give us license to destroy these fish. They were simply following their feeding instincts when they ate our baits and although we may consider this act bait stealing we have no right to impose the death penalty on the thief.

I suspect that the vast majority of surf fishermen seldom engage in any other aspect of the sport than bottom fishing. They find little enjoyment in the nocturnal habits of the plug caster, have no desire to walk out on a slippery jetty, and prefer to stay warm and dry even when a northeast blow is pushing big blues, stripers, or channel bass up on the beach. For many people, surf fishing is a form of relaxation. They may enjoy watching the sun rise over the ocean or just being on the beach during the quiet time between dusk and dark. Some may like the companionship of other fishers or just sitting in a beach chair and watching the people, especially those who look good in skimpy bathing suits, pass by. Bottom fishing fits this life-style like a hand in a glove. The tackle is simple, the action seldom interrupts your relaxation, and when you do catch something it is usually good to eat.

The Occasional Visitor

During my many years as a fishing reporter I have heard of some pretty spectacular catches from the surf. These include tarpon, swordfish, billfish, amberjack, cobia, tuna, and several other species usually associated with deeper offshore waters. More common are reports of

Spanish mackerel, little tunny, and king mackerel. Very few surf fishers actually set out to catch any of these fish, but it pays to be prepared for their unannounced arrival. You will find a large number of pier fishermen along the Atlantic Coast who do go after king mackerel, cobia, and tarpon using live baits on a trolly rig, but they don't qualify as surf casters.

Little tunny, or false albacore, is the most widely dispersed of these occasional visitors to the surf. It is one of the fastest-swimming game fish in the ocean but has absolutely no value as food. I have seen hungry cats walk away from a bowl of false albacore meat.

When a school of little tunny invades the surf you will need to make long and accurate casts if you have any plans to catch one. The object is to place the lure, usually a Hopkins or KastMaster, slightly in front of the feeding fish and then crank it in as fast as you possibly can. You locate your target by watching the birds. Generally, it won't be a big flock but just a half-dozen or so dipping and diving into the water. They move directly over the feeding fish, so a cast that lands in front of the birds should be on target.

There is one other aspect of the tunny feeding pattern that adds an even greater challenge to their capture. They feed on the move and as we mentioned earlier they move very fast. The angler must not only get his cast in front of the fish, but must also run down the beach trying to get himself ahead of them. A beach buggy or the stamina of a marathon runner is required to keep up with a school of little tunny. The standard procedure is to move down the beach until you are in position to intercept the school. If you are lucky you may get a half-dozen casts in before they move out of range again. Then the whole procedure repeats itself until you either hook up or run out of gas.

A false albacore hooked is a long way from a false albacore landed. The first run can strip your line down to a dangerous level. Then the fish will turn sideways to the beach and you will be fighting 15 to 20 pounds of tuna against a lot of ocean. Unfortunately, many of these fine fish fight to the point of exhaustion. Even so, they should be released because many will recover their strength.

Joe Malat of Nags Head, North Carolina, made one of the best catches of false albacore I have heard of. On a cold and quiet November morning Joe found a school of little tunny feeding along the beach just north of Oregon Inlet. He followed these fish almost back to Nags Head, catching and releasing five. He told me the conditions were ideal and he was the only angler working the school. A Hopkins No-Equal was the lure he used to compile this enviable record.

A Spanish mackerel is another speedster that can move in range of the surf caster. Once again, distance and accuracy are required to catch these fish, but the tackle is usually lighter because Spanish are smaller fish than false albacore. A fast retrieve is needed to lure them away from natural bait.

Warm, clear water is necessary to move the Spanish mackerel close to the beach. They often travel in large schools and are sometimes mixed with small bluefish. They will stay in one area for a reasonable period of time, so you don't have to chase them down the beach.

Small metal lures are the most effective method for capturing Spanish mackerel because they cast a longer distance than will a plug or bucktail. Spanish mackerel are usually about a cast-and-a-half off the beach, so a few extra feet can make a difference.

I have hooked two king mackerel from the surf but have yet to land one. These fish seldom get close enough for us to reach from the beach, but on both of those occasions there were large schools of bunker just beyond the breaking waves. You could see the big kings jumping clear of the water as they ripped into the bait. I hooked one on a Hopkins Shorty and the other on a live bunker I snagged out of the school. The first shook the hook and the second bit through the leader.

In some of the southern states surf anglers employ kites and balloons to get their live baits out where king mackerel, tarpon, and cobia roam. This requires an offshore breeze, but under the right circumstances I understand the results can be quite good. This method has resulted in hooking billfish along the Florida coast.

When offshore species such as tuna, amberjack, and billfish are landed in the surf it is usually an accident. Even in areas such as Montauk Point or Cape Cod, where tuna naturally move close to shore, the capture of one from the beach is a major news item. A few amberjack are taken each year around Cape Hatteras by some very surprised fishermen.

After you have been on the beach for a few seasons you will be able to detect when conditions are right for little tunny, Spanish mackerel, or other occasional visitors. This is the time to gear up for these fish so that you will be ready when they make an appearance. They don't stick around too long but they do provide some exciting fishing while they are near.

CHAPTER 8

MISCELLANEOUS EQUIPMENT

The more time you spend surf fishing, the more equipment you will accumulate. Some of this will prove valuable while a good many other acquisitions will end up collecting dust in your basement. All fishermen have a weakness for gadgets, and finding unusual items before anyone else on the beach has seen them is a part of our sport. Over the years I have collected my share of junk, but in the process I have uncovered some very useful equipment.

A pair of Berkley shears can be a valuable asset to your tackle collection. This tool incorporates a knife, scissors, bottle opener, screwdriver, bottle-cap remover, and several other such items into a single unit. It is particularly handy when preparing crab baits because you can easily snip the crab into sections with the powerful shears. The tool is well constructed and so far mine has shown no sign of rust.

Sand spikes are an important item for all surf casters. They come in a variety of sizes and are made from various materials. If you have a beach buggy, the weight of the sand spike will not be critical. I have one sand spike that is constructed from stainless steel and weighs several pounds. Most of my other spikes are made from schedule-40 PVC pipe, which is also quite heavy. I like a fairly long sand spike to hold the rod as high as possible above the waves and this length, when added to the thick pipe or heavy stainless steel, results in a spike with considerable weight.

Walk-on fishermen will require a lighter product that is easily car-

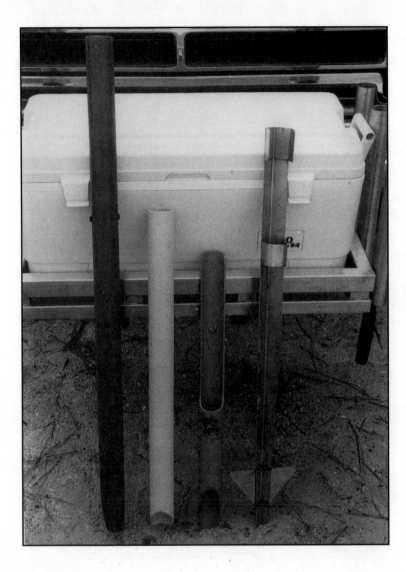

A variety of sand spikes are available to the surf fisher.

ried up on the beach. The best type of sand spike for this situation is made from thin-walled plastic pipe and is usually less than 3 feet long. You will find this type of spike in most coastal tackle shops and I have even seen them in K-Mart stores.

To make carrying them easier, you can drill a hole about an inch below the top and insert a piece of nylon or polypropylene rope. Tie the line to form a loop that you can slip over your shoulder to free your hands for carrying other items.

Sand spikes are handy not only for holding your rod while you fish but also for holding it while you bait up or tie on new rigs. Leaning a rod against your vehicle or on your beach chair will almost guarantee the reel a bath in the sand.

Most tackle boxes are not made for surf fishing. They don't have the room we need for big plugs and they suffer when loaded down with heavy sinkers. I have a Plano 747 box that does hold a fair number of big plugs and, so far, it has not failed to carry a heavy load of 4- to 6-ounce weights. I use smaller boxes made by Fenwick, Plano, and Flambeau to hold rubber lures, bucktails, snaps, hooks, and other items that would be lost in the bottom of the larger box. These small boxes can be removed and carried in your 5-gallon bucket when you walk on the beach.

Surf bags are also quite handy for walk-on fishermen. Most have canvas shells with aluminum or plastic dividers inside to keep your lures from becoming tangled. I keep my bag stocked with a few plugs, metal lures, bucktails, and ready-made leaders. I can grab it quickly and head up the beach to follow a school of blues or false albacore. It is also ready for a night trip on the jetty.

Those who fish at night will need some sort of portable light. The best light is one you don't have to hold in your hand but that can be carried on a strap around your neck or clipped to your jacket.

I have a light that resembles a miner's, and is powered by a battery pack clipped to my belt. The pack takes four D-size batteries, but I use the rechargeable type to cut down on the weight. This setup predates the new alkaline batteries, which last a long time in the most severe conditions, so if you don't mind additional weight they would work just as well as the rechargeables.

Panasonic makes a clip-on light with a goose neck that can be pointed in almost any direction. The beam is quite narrow but very bright, so it illuminates the area you are working on without lighting up the whole ocean.

The new high-intensity pen lights are very handy for the surf fisherman. The one I have is a Mity Lite made by Pelican but the Q Beam Lights work equally well. The light will clip on to your pocket but you must remove it to shine on your work area. I have held this light in my mouth while tying knots and this system works very well.

MISCELLANEOUS EQUIPMENT

The beam is so bright from this little flashlight that it safely lights the way for you to walk along unfamiliar beaches or rocky jetties.

Gaffs can come in handy on those glorious days when trophy fish invade the surf. Two basic types find favor with surf fishers. One is a small hand or release gaff attached to the angler via a coiled cord similar to the one on your telephone. The other is a long gaff that can be used when wading is not practical or desirable.

The small gaff is fine on a sloping beach where the angler and the fish are in close contact. The gaff is easy to carry and will be out of the way on your belt until it is needed. You will need a longer gaff when fishing from a jetty or from a beach where the drop-off is very sharp. You can't wade into the water from most jetties because the rocks are much too steep and slippery. You should not go in after the fish on a drop-off because in one step you can move from safe water into an area where the water is well over your head.

My gaff is made from an old fiberglass-rod blank. I have the gaff hook epoxied to one end and several wraps of cork tape for handholds on the butt. The gaff is 6 feet long and I can really reach out and touch someone when the occasion arises.

This long gaff is particularly handy for big bluefish. They will hang just beyond the wash on the other side of the break, putting a great deal of strain on your line and tackle. If you hoss them through the breakers you risk breaking them off or having them spit the hook as they tumble head first in the waves. With the long gaff you can walk down to the edge of the drop-off, reach over the waves, and get the fish. This procedure is best performed by two anglers, with one on the rod while the other gaffs the fish.

The long gaff is not easily carried but you can rig a nylon shock cord as a shoulder strap when fishing from a jetty or walking on the beach. Hook one end of the cord over the shaft of the rod and stretch it over your shoulder and under your arm. Now hook the other end of the cord to the butt of the gaff and it will stay in place and out of your way. All gaff points should be covered with pieces of tubing or other such devices when not in use.

A good pair of fishing gloves, such as those made by DuPont out of Kevlar fiber, can be very handy on the beach. I use them when cleaning fish to protect my hands and to keep a tight grip on the victim. The gloves also come in handy when you are bringing a big fish up the beach using the heavy mono or wire leader.

The longer you fish, the more necessary items you will collect, until you begin to move in the other direction and take a highly select group of gadgets with you. I have been fishing for over forty years and I am still collecting.

CHAPTER 9

COASTAL RUNDOWN

The object of this section will be to run down the Atlantic Coast states from Maine to Florida with an eye toward a few places in each state where the surf fisher can find easy access to the ocean. Some of these states have so much surf-fishing action and good surf-fishing spots that they could be the subjects of another book. Other states do not attract much attention from the surf caster due to a lack of trophy fish or difficulty in getting to the surf.

One of the advantages of surf fishing is the ease by which you can move from one place to another. Stow a pair of rods and some tackle in the car and you can be fishing a new spot as quickly as you can drive there.

Once you arrive you will find the state and federal park systems provide the best access to the beach. Unfortunately, there are many different fee systems and regulations governing the use of these parks, so it is a good idea to check with the ranger on duty before heading out on the beach.

Vehicle access is severely restricted or prohibited in many areas. In other jurisdictions you will find high permit fees or vehicle use will be restricted to residents only. Much of the National Seashore park system and many state-owned beaches were open to surf-fishing buggies, but once again, you should check with a local official before heading out.

Some of the more popular surf-fishing areas have guide-service operations where you can charter someone who will take you to the best spots at the best times. This is an excellent way to learn about a new fishing area, and when compared to a charter boat the cost is quite reasonable. Local tackle shops are the best source of up-to-date fishing information. They will also know about surf-fishing charter services and usually rent basic surf-fishing equipment.

The tackle shop will be your only supply of the local baits and lures that are currently catching fish. It has been my policy never to argue with the locals when it comes to fishing. They live there, fish there, and make their living off people who come there to fish. It is in their best interests to give you good reliable information. You may find a few of these people to be a bit rough around the edges and set in their ways, but their ways usually produce fish.

Maine and New Hampshire

According to Tim Coleman, editor of *New England Fisherman,* these are two of the most underutilized surf-fishing areas along the entire Atlantic Coast. Although their season is a bit shorter than states to the south, they still have good fishing for striped bass and bluefish during the summer. When you consider that most southern areas are in the doldrums at this time of year, a trip to these cool New England shores can be a welcome relief during July and August.

Striped bass have always been available here but, as with all other surf-fishing spots, the number of bass caught has declined. On the other hand, big bluefish were uncommon until the early 1980s, when they began to show up along the beach. No one can predict when the bass fishing will improve or when the blues will become scarce, but both of these species have a history of up-and-down population cycles.

Much of the surf fishing here is done with plugs, especially at night for striped bass. Baits such as live eels, mackerel, and porgies are also popular but become less attractive when big bluefish move into the surf.

Bottom fishing in the spring can produce cod but few people are out there due to the extreme cold conditions. In the summer some winter flounder are caught by bottom bouncers but not in any great numbers.

The folks at Saco Tackle in Kennebunkport recommended several access spots for surf fishing along the coast. The first was Scarboro

Beach State Park at Scarboro, Maine. There is ample parking during the day and you can secure permission at the local police station to park there at night if you are fishing.

Higgens Beach is another good fishing area but parking is available only at the grocery store across the street. The owner currently charges four dollars a day but he does keep a watch on the lot.

Popham Beach State Park is on the Kennebec River and provides access to some good fishing areas. The Biddeford Pool on Saco Bay has a public beach, bathhouse, and parking facilities. Parsons Beach State Park is also accessible with parking and good fishing opportunities.

There is no beach-buggy driving allowed on any of the public beaches in Maine. This is strictly a walk-on fishery, but with the good state park system you are assured of access.

The New Hampshire coast is the shortest on the Atlantic Seaboard. The same type of surf fishing is done here as in Maine and, according to Tim Coleman, it too is underutilized.

Massachusetts

I grew up reading about the fantastic surf fishing in Massachusetts. The stories written by Frank Woolner in *Salt Water Sportsman* told of big cow bass on night tides at Cape Cod, and I wanted to go. Unfortunately, it wasn't until the early 1970s that I had my first opportunity to fish the fabled waters.

On that first trip I was restricted to fishing the Cape Cod Canal because I did not have a beach buggy that would get me to the open surf on the Outer Cape. I plugged the canal and the nearby waters of Buzzard Bay and Sandwich Creek, catching a few mackerel but no striped bass. I finally resorted to bottom fishing with sandworms to put a few winter flounder in the cooler before heading home.

I was better prepared for my next trip because I had acquired my trusty Scout, and I headed for Provincetown where some other pilgrims landed a few hundred years before.

The first evening on the beach found me and my wife plugging the surf at Race Point. As the sun sat low on the water striped bass and bluefish hit the beach. We hooked up on every cast for over an hour and I felt like I was living a dream.

The stripers were small by Cape Cod standards, weighing under

20 pounds. The blues were big by anyone's standards, with many topping the 15-pound mark. It was a night to remember.

The next morning I returned to the same area to find the stripers gone but the blues thicker and bigger than ever. Every cast of my Hopkins produced an arm-wrenching strike and every blue I hooked was a monster. The wind came off the water and put a cold September chill in the air but I still have warm memories of that trip.

I have fished Nausset Beach near Orleans on nights when everyone on the beach, except me, landed at least one bass over 30 pounds. This is the only place where I have actually seen caught a striper over 50 pounds. The fish was taken at first light on a big Rebel plug. It was the first 50 that fisherman had caught, and the first one I had seen. We celebrated our good fortune with Jack Daniels out of Styrofoam cups at 6:00 A.M.

There have been many changes on Cape Cod over the years and few of them are for the good. Striped bass have declined in numbers but the big bluefish still show up. The beach that was once open to anyone who wanted to fish is closed in many areas to surf-fishing vehicles. Some of these closures were necessary due to beach erosion, but others were brought about due to the efforts of a group of preservationists who want to keep everyone off the beach.

You can still use your four-wheel-drive on the Cape but you should check with the park office at the Cape Cod National Seashore for permit requirements and areas that are open.

The Cape is not the only place to surf-fish in Massachusetts. There are some good areas between Plymouth and Newburyport, including Plum Island. I have never fished this section of beach but I suspect it also enjoys action from blues and bass.

For the most part, you will need fairly substantial tackle to fish the high surf in this state. Plug casting or working live eels are the most productive methods for taking stripers, and blues will hit both plugs and baits. Your rod should be able to cast a 3- or 4-ounce plug beyond the breakers and control a large fish once you have him hooked.

I have used lighter tackle in Buzzard Bay and at the mouth of Sandwich Creek on Cape Cod Bay, but neither of these areas are considered high surf.

The Cape Cod Canal provides a shortcut for ships and fish between Cape Cod Bay and Buzzards Bay. The current can run quite strong through here but the bigger bluefish and bass don't seem to mind. Big

162 SURF FISHING THE ATLANTIC COAST

plugs that make a commotion in the water will work well when the bigger fish are around.

I made one trip to Martha's Vineyard but never had a chance to fish. A great deal of the shoreline is controlled by private landowners, and access to the water is a problem. There is some public beach near Gay Head but parking is limited in this area. The Vineyard can be a great place to fish but you should make plans well in advance to be sure you have access to the beach.

Nantucket Island has a good deal of open beach and it can be an excellent place to surf-fish. Although I have never made the trip, I have spoken with several surf casters who think it is one of the greatest spots along the Atlantic Coast.

As with any beach, you have to read the water to find productive rips, holes, and sloughs, but there is plenty of structure on Nantucket. Because it is an island, the various combinations of tide and wind will create some good fishing conditions almost any time of day or night.

The Great Point is probably the most famous place to fish on Nantucket, but the ride out there is often as exciting as the fishing. According to my friends you can often find good fishing in areas that are much easier to get to.

Most of the surf fishing in Massachusetts is done from May to October, but bass and blues may stick around into early November. There is a cold-weather fishery for cod on the surf, but it does not draw nearly the number of participants as you will find pursuing the blues and bass.

Although the glory days of big stripers in the surf have waned, the beauty of Cape Cod remains the same. Many of us have worked hard to bring the striper back, and until they return we can catch blues and enjoy the scenery.

Rhode Island

This is the smallest state in the union but it has some very good surf fishing along its coast. There is fine structure from Watch Hill to Point Judith, and striped bass frequent these shores along with bluefish and a variety of bottom fish.

One of the most accessible areas is around Point Judith. You can fish the jetty at the inlet or the sand beach around to Point Judith Light. This is a natural harbor shaped like a bowl and game fish will move in to bottle up bait. Swimming plugs work well all along this stretch, especially on night tides. Bluefish will raid the beach during daylight hours in the fall as they stuff themselves with bait before the long hungry winter.

If you are looking for an entirely different type of fishing, take a trip to Block Island in October or November. This bustling summer resort becomes a fishing village after the tourists depart and it is one of the most picturesque places I have ever seen. But getting there is not easy. You must have a reservation on the ferry out of Point Judith if you plan to take your car. It is also a good idea to reserve a room on the island because many of the hotels are shut down this late in the season.

Another good reason to secure accommodations is the problems created by some surf fishers who try to come here and camp out on the beach or in local parking lots. Don't be surprised if you are met at the ferry landing by the local police and asked exactly where you plan to stay. Many Block Island residents don't appreciate itinerant fishermen taking up residence wherever they happen to land for the night.

There is very little tackle available on the island and food can be on the expensive side. Bring most of what you will need to fish and try to rent an efficiency apartment so that you can cook your own meals.

This is big striped bass country and you will need some sturdy tackle: a 10- to 12-foot rod, 15- to 20-pound line, and a strong reel with a very smooth drag. Plug casting is the favored technique with needlefish, the current favorite lure. Most of the fishing is done at night with anglers working one side of the island or another, depending on the wind and tide.

Big blues are likely to raid the beach in the fall, especially on the windward side of the island where bait has been blown in close to shore. Popping plugs or metal lures provide exciting action when conditions are favorable.

Much of the shoreline on Block Island and along the Rhode Island coast is very rocky. Bait fishing over this type of bottom is not easy because you often lose your rig in the rocks. If you fish bottom baits such as worms or squid, you will connect with winter flounder, tog, and other such bottom feeders.

While often overshadowed by its large sister states to the north and south, Rhode Island has surf fishing that is on a par with any state along the East Coast.

New York

Most of New York's surf-fishing activity takes place on Long Island. This large barrier island is one of the most populated areas on the East Coast, but in spite of this it still supports some very fine fishing opportunities.

The striped bass has always been the trophy fish for New York anglers. When they were in good supply during the 1960s and 1970s, most Long Island surf casters fished for nothing else. As the striper declined and bluefish increased, many anglers switched to blues while others remained fiercely loyal to the striper. A ban on commercial fishing for striped bass in the Hudson River has increased the population of these fish and increased the catches for Long Island anglers. The ban was recently increased to prohibit the sale of stripers anywhere in New York, which should help to further protect this species.

There are many access points for surf fishing along the Long Island shoreline. I have fished some of them but still rely on Fred Golofaro, editor of *Long Island Fisherman* magazine, to fill me in on most of the details. Fred has lived and fished on Long Island all his life and has a very good idea where you are likely to find fish.

The best places to try your luck would be the various state parks on Long Island. These places have access for those who use four-wheel-drive vehicles and parking for walk-on fishermen. Fishing from a state park insures easy access without the harassment you sometimes get from beachfront property owners who think they also own the ocean.

There are several state parks around Fire Island Inlet as well as the Fire Island National Seashore. You will need a state park permit to drive on the beach in any of the state parks plus another permit to drive on the national seashore. There are some beaches on Long Island that are controlled by Suffolk County and you must be a resident of the county to drive on these areas. All beaches are open to walk-on fishermen without a permit.

The state parks have another permit that allows anglers to park in the lots and fish the beaches after the park is officially closed. When you consider that most of the good striper fishing comes after dark, this permit can be very helpful.

Around Fire Island Inlet you will find Robert Moses, Cedar Beach, and Gilgo state parks. Running east from the end of Robert Moses Park is the Fire Island National Seashore, which provides many miles of open

The rocks at Montauk make an exciting fishing platform.

shoreline along the south beach. The Fire Island National Seashore has very strict limits on the number of vehicles allowed on the beach, but access to the state parks is a bit more liberal.

The east end of Long Island contains several state parks providing excellent surf-fishing opportunities. My personal favorite is Montauk Point State Park with its great fishing under the Lighthouse, in Turtle Cove, and off the North Bar. This particular area attracts a very devoted band of surf fishermen. These guys are not satisfied to fish near the water, they want to get into the water and wear wet suits so that they can withstand the cold water temperatures.

I have fished the North Bar on a cold night in October and watched as my friends disappeared into the dark water to return a few hours later dragging striped bass up to 35 pounds. In addition to the North Bar there are several large rocks within swimming distance of the beach and the wet-suit fishermen often use them.

It is a little drier under the lights but this area also has its hazards. The sheer drop to the water can make landing a big fish an exciting adventure. It can get a bit congested on the weekends, especially if the stripers, blues, or weakfish are in good supply.

Two other state parks on the east end are Hither Hills and Napeague. These are more traditional sand beaches as compared to the rocky shores around Montauk Point. Hither Hills offers some camping space and has a public bathing beach with a bathhouse.

Spring and fall are the best times to fish anywhere on Long Island,

166   SURF FISHING THE ATLANTIC COAST

but you will find reasonably good action even during the summer. School-sized stripers and bluefish move into the beach even during the hottest weather, with the best fishing at night or very early or late in the day.

Every time I visit Long Island I am amazed at how good the fishing is and how nice the beaches are this close to New York City. It is easy to forget that the largest metropolis in the world is only a few hours away when you are catching bass and blues under the Montauk Light.

New Jersey

This state has a very long coastline and a great deal of it is accessible to the surf fisher. Many people who are not familiar with New Jersey are unaware of its excellent fishing potential, but those of us who have been there know it compares favorably with almost any other state along the Atlantic Coast.

The point at Sandy Point State Park is a very good fishing area according to Dr. David Rockland, who grew up in this area. As a young man he worked in a major discount sporting goods store and when they closed up at 11:00 P.M. he would drive down to Sandy Point, park the car, and get a few hours sleep until it was time to fish.

David wanted to be on the Point before dawn, so he set out on the mile walk while it was still dark. First light usually brought in a school of blues or stripers that would hit surface poppers or swimming plugs. On those days when the blues or bass failed to show, David could rely on the fluke that hung around the deep drop-off at the Point. He still returns to this spot whenever he is in the area and reports fishing as good as it ever was.

Much of the New Jersey coast is lined with jetties. I have fished from and around them in Asbury Park on down to Cape May. All of this man-made structure will attract good numbers of fish, but some jetties seem to outproduce others. The better jetties not only draw in the fish but also attract large numbers of fishermen.

When big striped bass are in the surf you will find anglers working live bunker, herring, or eels from the jetties. During the 1970s, good numbers of bass over 50 pounds were taken using the live-bait method. Today, live bait still accounts for some big fish but the drastic reduction in the striped bass population has cut deeply into this style of fishing.

Many of the beaches along the North Jersey coast are controlled by the towns they border. Parking near the beach may be restricted or prohibited with tickets and tow-aways the punishment for those who ignore the rules. For those of us who grew up along the more isolated beaches of the south, it is strange to see an angler park his car and lock it on a city street, put some money in the meter, and then walk a block or two to the ocean.

Jerry Gomber, a New Jersey native who has fished all of these beaches for many years, likes to fish at Holgate whenever he can. Jerry says the beach is quite narrow with access by vehicle tightly restricted, but the deep holes and sloughs there can draw in some good-sized blues and striped bass.

Jerry is one of the few anglers I know who regularly fishes the surf with a fly rod. Under the right conditions he has taken blues and bass using the long wand. I have enough trouble casting a conventional surf stick, I don't need the added aggravation of a fly rod, but I must admit grudging admiration for Jerry and the others who can make it work. Holgate does provide the open space required to successfully cast a fly rod. Jerry also uses it at Long Beach Island where there is some competition from more conventional surf anglers.

The southernmost beach in New Jersey is Cape May. Here the Delaware Bay meets the Atlantic Ocean and some very good structure is created. There are a series of jetties around the Cape and, combined with the bars and holes along the ocean beach, you get a very fishy area. Big weakfish are the draw here as they take up summer residence around the jetties. Small swimming plugs or live baits worked close to the rocks will usually draw them out.

There are a number of beaches along the Jersey Shore that allow you to use your surf-fishing vehicle for a fee. Some of the beaches are controlled by the local towns and others are controlled by the state. Buying a pass or permit for every beach will cost you several hundred dollars, so most surf casters pick one or two favorites and restrict their fishing to those spots.

Delaware

Surf fishing is easily accessible along the entire Delaware coastline. There are a few areas of so-called private beach in front of exclusive developments, but you still have the right to fish the beaches, although no one ever bothers to try.

Cape Henlopen is the northernmost ocean beach and it is a prime fishing location. The Delaware Bay and Atlantic Ocean meet off this point and the result of this mixing is myriad bait and game fish.

Sea trout or weakfish are the trophy fish of the Delaware coast and if they show up anywhere at all it will be at Cape Henlopen. The strong current and wave action around the point cut deep sloughs between shallow bars and the weakfish use this bottom structure to their advantage. They push bait into these areas or wait for the current to move it there and then they commence to have a feast.

This same pattern also attracts bluefish, which have been more abundant in recent years than have the trout. Big blues show up in the spring and fall, while the smaller version can be taken during the summer. The best of the sea-trout fishing will be in October and November.

There are large parking lots throughout Cape Henlopen State Park with the one at the Radar Tower most convenient for walk-on fishermen. Parking is free, except during the summer between Memorial Day and Labor Day, when a small fee is charged. You will need a permit to drive on any of the Delaware beaches and these are not so reasonable. The current rate is forty dollars for residents of Delaware and eighty dollars per year for nonresidents.

As you drive south on the beach you will find a jetty about 2 miles before the point. This is called the Navy Beach and it can be productive for blues and trout.

Rehoboth is the biggest town on the Delaware coast and you can fish all along this beach unless the lifeguards are on duty. There is an old barge sunk close to the beach on the south side of town and this can be a good fishing spot if you don't mind losing a few rigs.

As a boy I spent my summer vacations in Rehoboth and we always stayed at the Mary Ann Inn on Olive Avenue. In the evening I would wander up on the beach and watch the surf fishermen with their Calcutta rods, Ocean City reels, and linen line. Captain Ball, who was also our neighbor back home, was particularly proficient with this equipment and quite patient with an inquisitive kid. This was my introduction to surf fishing and I am still an inquisitive kid who remains fascinated by it all.

Parking is available on the streets of Rehoboth and its neighbor to

A picket line of anglers works the Delaware surf.

the south, Dewey Beach. In the spring and fall you can park very close to the beach but in the summer you are lucky to find a spot in town.

A few years ago the mayor of Rehoboth decided to ban surf fishing on the town's beach. This proposal upset so many people, especially those who had retired to Rehoboth so that they could fish, that no work could be done in the mayor's office because the phone would not stop ringing. It rang just as loud at the offices of town council members and even in the governor's office. It still took two days for the mayor to decide that his proposal probably would not work.

The Delaware Sea Shore State Park runs most of the way from Dewey Beach down to Bethany Beach. Several parking areas are available and you can drive along most of this beach. Indian River Inlet divides this park in half and the North Pocket at the inlet is another very good fishing hole. You can park very close by, so walk-on fishermen have easy access. There is a state-owned campground on the south side of the inlet that is inhabited by fishers in the spring and fall.

The best fishing in the North Pocket occurs when the wind blows down the beach from the north. This pushes bait and game fish in between the jetty and the beach, giving surf casters and jetty jockies an equal chance. Fall is the best time to fish here as big blues and trout move in to feed on spot and mullet.

The southernmost fishing beach on the Delaware coast is Fenwick Island. There is a large state park here with a big parking lot and access for surf vehicles. This beach seldom develops any particular structure and has a gradual slope without much of a drop-off. In spite of this, you can do very well here on small fish during the summer and big blues or trout in the fall.

There are several tackle shops along Delaware Route 1 that specialize in surf fishing, but there are no guide services available. Bait is usually available until late November and some shops will stay open in December if the fish are still around.

Maryland

When I was a youngster, the beach from the Delaware state line down to Ocean City was long, wide, and open to surf fishing. Today, Ocean City begins at the Delaware state line and there are condos, apartments, and hotels lined along the beach. The beach has also lost a great deal of its width and in 1988 the state began a replenishment program to pump sand from the ocean floor up to the beach. Only time will tell how long this widened beach will last.

Fishing from the beach is still permitted in Ocean City, but for the most part it is done by residents or those who rent beachfront units for their vacations. No driving is permitted on the beach and street parking is at a premium. You can find a space to park during the off-season and this is when surf fishing is at its peak.

Most surf fishers will take the extra time to drive down to Assateague Island and leave the condo crowd in Ocean City. Assateague is a beautiful place with sea oats, dunes, and wild ponies on a long expanse of open beach. You can fish anywhere along the island but only the federal park to the south is open to surf vehicles. You will need a permit for your buggy that you can purchase at the park office just before you cross the bridge onto the island. There is a day permit for ten dollars or a year-long permit for thirty dollars.

There is a sand road behind the dunes with several access ramps to the beach. Good fishing can be available anywhere along the beach depending on how the surf makes up. The shifting tides and currents create bars and sloughs that change quite frequently. You must reexamine the structure every time you go up there, and locate the holes, bars, and sloughs that have developed since your last visit.

Assateague is situated between the north and the south, so it gets some specimens from each area. Bluefish and trout remain the stable species, but you may encounter kingfish, spot, croaker, spotted sea trout, channel bass, and false albacore. Spanish and king mackerel are not common, but they do stop by for an occasional visit.

When striped bass were more plentiful we used to open the season each spring with a trip to Assateague for some rockfish. Bloodworms would attract these fish, most of which were under 10 pounds, but I always hoped for that elusive cow bass.

Camping is available in both the state and federal parks. Walk-on fishers will find parking lots closer to the surf for their convenience.

The summer crowds are very heavy at Assateague and on holiday weekends access may be closed due to overcrowding. Fishing is better and there is a lot more room on the island in the spring and fall.

There are several bait and tackle shops in Ocean City, but most surf fishers stop by Shockley's Store before they go out on the island. Bill Shockley is an avid surf fisherman who will be happy to advise the novice angler.

Virginia

You can fish almost the entire length of the Virginia coast but you will have to work a little harder to reach the majority of this very productive surf. The only areas with easy access are Assateague Island in the north and Sandbridge in the south. You can fish the surf at Virginia Beach but, like Ocean City, it is used primarily by those who own or rent property along the strip.

The Virginia portion of Assateague Island is part of the Assateague National Seashore and the same permit that allows you to drive on the Maryland portion is also valid here. They have provided a good deal of parking all along the beach and it probably has better access for walk-on fishermen than most other areas along the coast.

The Point at Tom's Cove is a favorite fishing spot because big blues and other game fish will wait along here to ambush bait moving out of the bay. Most of the beach from here to the Maryland line is quite flat with little structure. A portion of this beach is a designated Wilderness Area where human intrusion is closely controlled.

The rest of the coast from Assateague down to Fisherman's Island is completely isolated from the mainland by a series of bays that have never known a bridge piling. There are twelve barrier islands, many of which are controlled by the Virginia Coast Preserve. The other islands are owned by the state or federal government with only Cedar and parts of Hog Island still in private hands. This is the last frontier of natural beaches left on the Atlantic Coast. The development that destroyed the other barrier islands has been stopped here and I hope it is never allowed to infringe.

To fish on these islands you will need a boat. I use a 14- to 16-foot aluminum skiff that will run across the shallow bays and can be dragged up on the beach while I fish. Many local anglers use a Chincoteague Scow because it is designed to navigate these waters better than any other craft.

There are a number of good public boat ramps along the mainland, so access to the islands is not a problem. Most of my fishing has been on Hog, Wreck, Myrtle, Cobb, and Smith islands, but I know other anglers who do well on Cedar and Metompkin. Parramore Island is still controlled by the original owners and Ship Shoal is off limits due to live ordnance left over from its days as a bombing target.

The structure of these islands is constantly changing. There are no jetties, bulkheads, snow fences, or any other man-made intrusions on the natural makeup of the beach. Each trip to the barrier islands requires a new assessment of the beach to find promising structure.

My favorite island in this chain is Hog. I have caught good numbers of both red and black drum here and it is fairly easy to reach out of Quinby, where they have a good but lightly used boat ramp.

The run out to Hog Island follows a deep channel to Quinby Inlet. It is a bit on the narrow side from Quinby Harbor to the junction with the Intercoastal Waterway, so be sure to follow all navigational aids.

You can anchor your boat on the north end of the island or pull it up on the beach. Be sure to tie it securely so that it will be there when you return.

There are no bait and tackle shops or grocery stores on any of these islands so you must carry everything you will need to survive the day with you. This can be quite a task unless you learn to travel light. Don't try to take everything out of your beach buggy. I find two rods and reels, some rigs and sinkers, bait, sandwiches, water, and a few lures will see me through. A VHF radio and a first aid kit can come in handy should an emergency arise.

On Hog Island there is a point of sorts that develops south of

A lone angler casts alongside the pier at Sandbridge, Virginia.

Quinby Inlet, but exactly how far south will depend on the latest change in the beach created by the most recent storm. This point has provided me with the best red drum fishing I have ever experienced. On two separate occasions I have caught drum on every cast, using peeler-crab baits.

The best time for drum fishing here is late May to early June. The fish show up again in September and may hang around until early October. Big blues arrive ahead of the drum in the spring and will be back again in October and November. Bottom fish round out the year with some excitement from Spanish mackerel and false albacore in late summer or early fall.

The bird life on Hog and all of the other barrier islands is spectacular. There are nesting colonies of terns, skimmers, and other seabirds, plus rookeries loaded with herons and egrets. Man's intrusion is evidenced by feral cattle on Hog Island and an overabundance of rabbits on Cobb. The islands were once used as natural corrals by local farmers.

The Nature Conservancy encourages fishing from these islands but they do ask you to observe a few rules. You may not camp overnight, drive a vehicle on the beach, bring along any domestic animals, or harass the birds or wildlife on the islands. You must leave the islands exactly as you find them by taking all litter back to the mainland. These are the true treasures along our coast but are easily spoiled by the thoughtless actions of visitors.

The southernmost beach on the Virginia coast is Sandbridge, in the city of Virginia Beach. There is a fishing pier here and plenty of parking for walk-on fishermen but the structure of the beach is rather flat with little to hold the attention of fish. They do get a run of big blues in the spring and fall with a variety of bottom fish available in the summer.

Some surf fishing does take place around Rudee Inlet and along the Resort Strip of Virginia Beach. Here too the beach offers little structure but there are a few bars located within casting distance at some locations.

Blues and sea trout provide excitement when they show up in the spring and fall with spot, croaker, and sea mullet available during the rest of the season. Most of the fishermen who work these waters are vacationers staying at the local motels and hotels. Resident anglers will usually drive down to Sandbridge where access is much easier.

North Carolina

No other state along the Atlantic Coast provides better access to great surf-fishing opportunities than North Carolina. From the northern-most beaches at Duck and Corolla down to Salter Path on the Bouge Banks, you can fish almost anywhere you choose. Some spots are naturally better than others, but even a rundown of all the good fishing areas is too lengthy for this effort. We will touch on a few of the places where I have found success, but rest assured there are many others available to the surf fisher who is willing to travel.

Oregon Inlet provides excellent fish-holding structure and is easy to access either by vehicle or by walk-on fishermen. The south side of the inlet is slowly washing away and the beach gets closer to the parking lot each year. Just the opposite is true of the north side, where a wide expanse of very flat beach stretches from the road to the ocean.

You don't need any type of vehicle permit to drive on the beach of Cape Hatteras National Seashore as this is written, but I do expect some type of fee and inspection system to be in place in the very near future. This is the last free-access beach in the National Park System and the government hates a free ride almost as much as nature hates a vacuum.

The structure of the inlet is constantly changing, but the north side usually has an outer bar at the mouth and some good deep holes farther up the beach toward Nags Head. At times there will be a pool or pocket created at the north end of the inlet where blues and other game fish will drive bait. This can provide some fantastic action for those anglers who are lucky enough to be there when the blitz occurs.

The action of the ocean and the current from the inlet has cut a very deep edge along the south side of the inlet. If you park in the lot provided behind the Coast Guard station, you can fish this edge without walking more than a few yards.

Flounder and spotted sea trout are the most popular fish here but you are likely to find blues, spot, sea mullet, and most any other fish common to these waters along this edge at any given time. I know of no other surf-fishing spot that is so easily reached by walk-on fishermen and yet it provides some of the best fishing along the entire Atlantic Coast.

The Point at Cape Hatteras is legend among surf casters, but its popularity may be its undoing. When a bluefish or drum blitz is in progress the crowds not only are enormous but also contain some of the most ill-behaved fishermen I have ever encountered. There are those who believe the ocean and the beach are their personal domain and the rest of us are no more than trespassers. For some reason The Point seems to attract more than its share of these characters, and when they all try to fish the same spot fireworks often erupt.

In spite of the hazards, there is no more fishy water anywhere than here. The Diamond Shoals make the perfect backdrop as waves explode 20 feet or more in the air and birds dive on the bait stirred up by this violent action. The water is very deep and drops off sharply on the south side of The Point, while the north beach has a more gradual slope. Big drum and bluefish tend to move into the south side on a southwest wind and the north side when the wind blows from that direction.

In the summer small bluefish and Spanish mackerel will chase bait around The Point when the water is clear. Cobia and tarpon are occasionally hooked during the warmer months. Flounder, croaker, spot, and sea mullet are available almost year-round. Spotted sea trout and pompano generally avoid the fast water at The Point and are more likely to show up on the South Beach behind the campground or on the North Beach by the lighthouse.

Every surf fisher should experience The Point at Cape Hatteras, if only to observe the phenomenon. I leave the choice of whether to fish there or not up to you.

My favorite area to fish Cape Hatteras is the beach north of Avon. The crowds are not as heavy and the pressure is not so intense, so you can enjoy your sport without fighting to hold your place on the beach. There are a series of deep holes protected by sandbars all along this beach. You can ride along looking for fish action or just pick out a likely looking spot and wait for something to come to you.

This section of beach is best during the fall when blues and drum are moving south but it also produces in the spring if the wind keeps the fish close to the beach. David Deuel caught his world-record drum here in the fall of 1984.

There are several parking areas and access ramps between Rodanthe and Avon, but walk-on anglers will need a good set of legs to make the trip over the dunes. Many people do walk on, but those who have beach buggies are in the majority.

One of the major benefits of Cape Hatteras is that the entire area is geared for the fisher. All the local businesses cater to anglers and there are guide services that specialize in taking visitors surf fishing. The tackle-shop owners are knowledgeable and don't hesitate to put you on to the latest location of sure hot action. Restaurants serve early breakfasts and late dinners, catering to the hours of the surf fisher. Once you get past Nags Head you will have a hard time finding tennis courts, golf ranges, swimming pools, or shopping malls. When you come here, you come to fish.

There are some islands south of Cape Hatteras that are noted for their excellent surf fishing. Ocracoke and Portsmouth are two of the most popular and both are accessible by ferry. You reach Ocracoke Island from the ferry at the south end of Hatteras Island. It is a short crossing and the boat sails on a regular schedule.

Ocracoke has all of the amenities the traveling angler will need, including bait, tackle, ice, gas, restaurants, motels. Portsmouth Island is uninhabited, so you must carry all the necessities with you. Access to Portsmouth is via a private ferry service. There are a few cabins on the island that you can rent, or you can camp out on your own.

The final beach we will examine in North Carolina is east of Morehead City on Emerald Isle. I camped and fished here near the town of Salter Path in the late 1960s. Fishing was very good in the summer for sea mullet, croaker, gray trout, and pompano. The beach has some very good structure with a long outer bar protecting some very deep holes and sloughs close to the beach.

Emerald Isle has acquired a considerable number of homes and condos over the last twenty years, but fishing remains quite good. The big bluefish and drum blitzes common on Hatteras Island and other beaches to the north don't often occur down here, but the bottom fishing is good so you seldom go home empty-handed.

South Carolina and Georgia

I have never fished the surf anywhere in these two states. I have done some fishing in the lakes of South Carolina but have yet to wet a line in Georgia.

In order to find out about surf-fishing opportunities in this area I contacted Don Millus, a resident of South Carolina and a book author. Don has fished all along the Southeast Coast and especially enjoys surf fishing.

According to Don, the Myrtle Beach section of the South Carolina coast offers the greatest opportunity for the surf fisherman. There is very good access from many roads for the walk-on fisher, but all four-wheel-drive use of the beach is severely restricted. A few sections of beach are open in the winter but for the most part you can consider the beaches closed to all vehicles.

The beach along this section of coast is sandy with a very gradual slope and no outer bar. This lack of natural structure makes finding fish a bit difficult, so most surf fishermen concentrate their efforts near inlets, piers, or other man-made structure.

One of Don's favorite spots is Cherry Grove Inlet north of Myrtle Beach. Here you will find good access and a chance to catch small channel bass or spotted sea trout. Channel bass or red drum are known as spot-tailed bass in South Carolina and Georgia. These fish seldom reach the 50-pound mark down here, but at 10 or 15 pounds they still represent the biggest fish a surf angler is likely to encounter.

The spotted sea trout is another trophy catch for surf fishers in this area. In the late fall and early winter they are taken on shrimp or on Mirro-Lures by anglers who often wade in the shallow water close to the beach.

The rest of the fish taken on the surf are small bottom feeders. High on the list are sea mullet and pompano. Live sandfleas, or mole crabs, are the top baits for both of these fish. Snapper blues are likely to show up at any time, especially on a high tide. A few flounder are captured each year with most of them coming from the inlets or near jetties.

Due to the gentle surf and small fish you can usually fish with light tackle along this coast. Don recommends an Ambassador 5000 reel matched to an 8-foot rod. A one-handed spinning outfit works best when you are using Mirro-Lures for spotted trout.

Other favorite spots for surf fishing include the Second Avenue Pier, which attracts trout and pompano. The jetty at Huntington Beach State Park south of Murrells Inlet has good surf fishing and is also a good place to take the family for a day on the beach. The south jetty has a very flat top and a king mackerel or two are taken from the end each year.

The mouth of Winyah Bay near Georgetown is a good fishing spot but you will need a boat to get there. You can put your boat in at the launch ramp in Georgetown, then motor down to the inlet. Surf fishing is good in the ocean, bay, and directly in the inlet.

In southern South Carolina Don recommends Hunting Beach State Park. Here you have easy access to a public beach.

There are many islands all along the South Carolina and Georgia coasts, and you can fish from most of them if you can get out there. In fact, all of the productive surf fishing in Georgia is off these islands, but access is definitely a problem.

You will need a small boat. Don suggests a 14- or 16-foot aluminum skiff with a suitable outboard motor. A chart of the area where you plan to fish is a necessity and Don strongly recommends a guide if you are not familiar with these waters.

Once you get to the island you will find the same sandy, gently sloping beach and the same variety of fish as in South Carolina. The channel bass will most likely show up near the inlets with the bottom fish available in most any location.

While not the hotbed of surf-fishing activity you find in North Carolina, South Carolina and Georgia provide some fish and a less hectic beach.

Florida

Florida has one of the longest coastlines of any state in the nation, but surf fishing is not as popular here as it is in areas where large fish are attracted to the beach. Much of the Florida surf is shallow with a smooth sand bottom, great for bathing but not so good for fishing. Many would-be surf anglers end up on the end of a pier in order to reach water deep enough to hold larger fish.

I have fished the surf around Mayport, Florida, at the mouth of the Saint Jones River. Working from the jetty, I caught Spanish mackerel on Jerk Jigger lures but had no luck at all when fishing from the beach.

Since my Florida surf fishing was quite limited, I contacted Vic Dunaway, editor of *Florida Sportsman* magazine, and asked for his opinion on the best places to fish along the Florida coast. Vic said you can fish almost anywhere, but your catch generally will be limited to small bottom fish.

The one exception comes in April and May, when good-sized bluefish push bait into the surf and anglers have a field day. Several years ago they had a run of big chopper blues weighing 15 pounds or more, but fish of that size are now quite rare.

Channel bass are also taken from the surf, with most of this action taking place around inlets. Sebastian Inlet is a good spot to try your luck on the channel bass, or "reds," as they are known in Florida.

Hutchinson Island off Route A1A is another good surf-fishing spot, according to Vic. There is plenty of access and the fishing is steady if not spectacular.

While surf fishing is not extremely popular in Florida, bank and bridge fishing enjoys a large following. It is hard to find a bridge that doesn't have a few folks fishing from the rails or from the bank adjoining the span. When you have a beach without much fish-holding structure, the fish will move to man-made structure. The deep holes and rips created around bridge pilings will be considerably better fishing spots than will a featureless beach.

The traveling surf fisher who plans to spend some time in Florida would be well advised to carry a 7- or 8-foot rod matched to a reel full of 10- to 12-pound line, and confine his fishing to bridges, piers, and banks. This is not to say that fish can't be taken from the beach, but unless you are in the right place at the right time when the big blues show up you just won't need any heavy tackle.

Fishing from the Florida beach will probably be best on high tides. This will bring the fish in with the deeper water and you will have a better chance of catching something.

Since most of the action will be from small fish, stick with small baits and hooks. Sandfleas are popular baits, along with cut mullet, shrimp, and squid. Hooks should be 1/0 or smaller.

Put your bait just outside the breakers and work it back to the beach. The action of the waves will stir up the bottom, dislodging small baits that will attract fish. Without heavy bottom structure this wave action becomes the only fish attraction on the beach.

INDEX